cookielicious™

150 FABULOUS RECIPES TO BAKE & SHARE

BY FOOD EDITOR JANET K. KEELER
St. Petersburg Times

FOREWORD BY JOHN MARIANI

BOOK DESIGN BY NIKKI LIFE

Copyright © 2010 Times Publishing Company and Seaside Publishing
Photography Copyright © 2010 by Times Publishing Company

150 FABULOUS RECIPES TO BAKE & SHARE

BY JANET K. KEELER

Publisher: Joyce LaFray
Designer: Nikki Life
Senior Editor: Patricia Mack
Editor: Jeanne Grinstead
Photographers: Scott Keeler, Patty Yablonski (cookie photos), Cherie Diez (author photo)
Technical Support: Dallas K. Jones, Jacob Parker, Susannah Green

All rights reserved. No part of this work may be reproduced or transmitted in any form or by any means, electronic or mechanical including photocopying, recording, or by any information storage and retrieval system without permission in writing from the publisher. Requests for permission should be addressed to:
Permissions Department, Seaside Publishing, P.O.Box 14441, St. Petersburg, Florida 33733

Library of Congress Cataloging-in-Publication Number: 2010934422
ISBN: 978-0942084-34-4

Printed in the United States of America
First Edition
10 9 8 7 6 5 4 3 2 1

Toll Free Orders & Special Sales: 1-888-FLA-BOOK (888-352-2665)
www.timescookierecipes.com

Cover Photo: Peanut Lover Chocolate Cookies by Scott Keeler, recipe on page 165.

dedication

To my parents, Dick and Fran Krietemeyer,
who gave me the best start ever
and taught me how to love a child.
And for Richard and Susan, who always
indulged and put up with their little sister.

acknowledgements

A super-size thank you to the loyal readers of the St. Petersburg Times food section who graciously shared their favorite cookie recipes and the memories that go with them. Their enthusiasm for our annual cookie project has never waned.

Many of my colleagues at the Times have contributed their creative energies, too, and without them, this book would not have been possible. I am indebted to chief cookie tester and recipe interpreter Karen Pryslopski, who knows how difficult it is to find candied cherries in September. She is the backbone of the book. For the past decade, Patty Yablonski has made me laugh at myself when I took things too seriously, plus photographed nearly every cookie on these pages.

I'm thankful to designer Nikki Life, who always has lessons to teach about how to make things look better and make more sense to readers. She pushes us toward perfection, something I need. My friend, colleague and cooking muse Lennie Bennett is always super supportive and ready with a willing ear.

Thank you also to the many designers and copy editors who improve my work and make readers take notice. I am grateful to the many journalists who tested cookies over the years, proving that everyone loves cookies even if their main beat is covering city hall. Thanks for the last-minute assistance from Jan Brackett, B Buckberry, Holly and Andy Braford, Jennifer DeCamp and Barbara Moch. Without them we wouldn't have a photo for every recipe.

It is wonderful to work for a company that supports creative endeavors, and the St. Petersburg Times is that kind of place. I've been fortunate to work there since 1992.

My husband, Scott, gets a big, sugary kiss. He is my partner in all things, including work. His creative talents and patience are a thread throughout the book. And lastly, thank you to our son, Jensen, who cheerfully eats the broken cookies so we can save the good ones for the photos. He is smart, witty and a good sport.

JANET K. KEELER

contents

foreword

BY JOHN MARIANI

For many people a single cookie is a guilty pleasure; for others six are a mere indulgence. But whatever the number, the sheer joy derived from nibbling cookies is universal, whether it's a fig cookie in Istanbul or a shortbread cookie in Scotland.

There seems no end to their variety—whether they are glazed, fudgy, filled with nuts, studded with chocolate, topped with coconut, or layered with marshmallow. There are seasonal cookies and holiday cookies, campfire cookies and cookies stacked in painted tins and pink paper. All these, old-fashioned and newfangled, are contained in Janet K. Keeler's ebullient collection of cookies that share one thing in common — they look, smell, crack, break apart, crumble and delight, from the moment you lay eyes on them. Some melt on the tongue, others stick to the roof of your mouth. There is chocolate galore, from chewy chocolate macaroons with meringue to decadently rich Death by Chocolate.

Janet, who has won a number of well-deserved prizes for her writing at the St. Petersburg Times and served as a Pillsbury Bake-Off judge, has spent a decade compiling, testing and reworking cookie recipes to reflect their infinite diversity, and she is the first to credit the hundreds of people who over those years have sent her beloved family recipes to share with readers. I imagine many of those recipes date back to the 19th century and early 20th century, when America became cookie mad, creating regional classics ranging from brownies and blondies to Joe Froggers and hermits, from gingersnaps to snickerdoodles, from Toll House chocolate chip to s'mores.

The mere aroma of cookies baking in a hot oven can bring people to tears of nostalgia for Christmas cookies scented with nutmeg and cinnamon, ginger and mace. Indeed, it was the memory of a cookie — the butter-rich madeleine — that caused French author Marcel Proust to go off and write nine volumes of memoirs entitled In Remembrance of Things Past. Who can name any other food with that kind of propelling power?

Janet's cookies partake of that power to make a person swoon. I suppose there is such a thing as a bad cookie but you won't find any in this collection. Look at any of the photos: These are not dainties, they are what you want to grab a handful of, sniff and savor, nibble away, dip in milk or coffee or tea and feel just as happy as you did when a cookie was a reward for good behavior.

JOHN MARIANI IS FOOD AND TRAVEL COLUMNIST FOR *ESQUIRE MAGAZINE* AND AUTHOR OF *THE ENCYCLOPEDIA OF AMERICAN FOOD & DRINK*.

introduction

START YOUR MIXERS!

Cookies have power. They bring people together more than any other sweet treat. Maybe it's the communal nature of the platter, but when a plate of homemade cookies appears, people gather in high excitement.

The beauty of cookies is that they are not difficult to make. This book is filled with delicious, doable recipes fit for home cooks of all skill levels. Whether you like chocolate or citrus, nuts or dried fruit (or maybe all of that in one cookie), you'll find a recipe to suit your fancy. You won't need exotic equipment to succeed, and nearly all ingredients are readily available in grocery stores across the country. There's also a measure of flexibility. Although nuts and cookies are natural partners, they can be omitted from most of the recipes with good results.

Homemade is good, frustration is not. If you're anything like me, finding time to make cookies can be rough. That's why I've noted the "freezeworthiness" of each recipe. I like to bake ahead when I have time and I am sure the same is true for you.

The majority of "Cookielicious™" cookies came from the recipe boxes and Web stashes of St. Petersburg Times' readers. They are their favorites and over the years have become some of mine, too. I have tinkered with a few and renamed others to better describe the goodness that awaits. I've tasted every single one and can vouch for the wow-factor. All you need do is pick recipes that speak to you. I suspect there will be many.

In the decade since I started an annual cookie project, I have received about 5,000 recipes via e-mail and snail mail, many painstakingly written by hand. That's certainly a testament to our love affair with the cookie. The passion of home cooks has helped me inspire a new generation of bakers.

We all share the "cookielicious" joy of delicious homemade cookie recipes. Now, to the kitchen!

Janet K. Keeler

CHAPTER 1

ANYTIME

COOKIE JAR TREATS TO TEMPT FRIENDS AND FAMILY OF ALL AGES

There's something comforting about having a full cookie jar in the house, or a container of favorite cookies in the freezer. They are the sweet pick-me-up that is so welcome after a rough day at work or hectic hours with the kids.

And isn't it nice to be able to offer a treat when a neighbor has dropped by to share good news or is in need of a sympathetic ear? A few cookies on a plate served with a steaming cup of tea or coffee, or a glass of ice cold milk, make everything better.

The cookie recipes in this chapter are not difficult to make, but are special enough to let everyone know you cared enough to turn butter, sugar, flour and eggs into something fantastic. No need to wait for a special occasion. Cookies can be enjoyed anytime.

ANYTIME! COOKIES

Hawaiian Delights

PHOTO ON PAGE 118

MAKES: 2 dozen.

FREEZEWORTHY: Yes, but cool completely first.

NOTES

Everyone will say "mahalo" (thank you) after biting into these tropical treats. And you'll be happy they start with refrigerated cookie dough.

1 (18-ounce) package refrigerated sugar cookie dough
1 cup coarsely chopped macadamia nuts (salted or unsalted)
1 cup sweetened shredded coconut

Preheat oven to 350 degrees.

Mix ingredients in bowl with a fork. Drop rounded tablespoon mounds of mixture onto ungreased cookie sheet about 2 inches apart.

Bake for 12 to 14 minutes, or until golden. Cool on baking rack.

KANDI J. GARTLEY

TIP *Before baking an entire batch of cookies, bake one or two cookies to see how much they spread on the baking sheet. If they spread more than you'd like, try refrigerating the dough until well chilled, one to two hours.*

Mocha Macadamia Shortbread

PHOTO PAGE 116

MAKES:
4 dozen.

FREEZEWORTHY:
Yes, but without icing. Let thaw and come to room temperature before icing.

NOTES

These shortbread cookies are flavored by pulverized macadamia nuts and then frosted with coffee-flavored icing. A special treat for a job promotion!

¾ cup (3½ ounces) salted macadamia nuts
⅔ cup sugar
½ teaspoon vanilla
1 cup (2 sticks) unsalted butter, cut into half-inch pieces
2¼ cups all-purpose flour

MOCHA GLAZE:
1 tablespoon instant coffee granules
3 tablespoons boiling water
4 tablespoons butter, melted
1¾ cups confectioners' sugar, sifted
1 teaspoon vanilla

To make the cookies, place the macadamia nuts and sugar in a food processor and pulse for about 30 seconds or until the mixture resembles a fine meal. Add the vanilla and butter. Process just until smooth. Add 1¼ cups of the flour and pulse just until the flour is incorporated. Stir in the remaining cup of flour and process just until the dough starts to form a ball. Briefly knead the dough to fold in any loose crumbs.

Divide the dough in half and shape each half into a log about 8-inches long on a sheet of waxed paper or plastic wrap. Tightly wrap the dough and twist the ends closed. Chill for several hours or overnight.

Preheat the oven to 350 degrees; set rack in the middle of the oven.

Cut the chilled dough into ⅓-inch-thick slices and place 1 inch apart on ungreased baking sheets. Bake for 8 to 9 minutes or just until set but not brown. Let the cookies cool on the baking sheet for a few minutes, and then transfer them to a wire rack (careful, they're fragile while they're still warm).

To make glaze, dissolve the coffee in boiling water. Whisk in the melted butter, confectioners' sugar and vanilla, mixing until smooth. Cover the glaze with plastic wrap, with the wrap actually touching the surface, until ready to use.

Glaze the cookies while still warm using a pastry brush. For less sweet cookies, drizzle the glaze over cookies. Store completed cookies in an airtight container to retain crispness.

JANET K. KEELER

Apricot Bars

PHOTO ON PAGE 117

MAKES:
About 35 bars.

FREEZEWORTHY:
So-so results; jam may get runny when thawed.

NOTES

Substitute another flavor of jam and you'll have a completely different bar. Think peach, strawberry, raspberry, blackberry and even mango.

1¼ cups quick-cooking rolled oats (not instant)
2 cups all-purpose flour
1 cup brown sugar
1 cup (2 sticks) unsalted butter or margarine, melted
1 teaspoon baking soda
½ teaspoon salt
1 (18-ounce) jar apricot jam

Preheat oven to 350 degrees.

Blend all ingredients, except jam, to crumb-like consistency. Reserve 1½ cups for topping. Press remainder into ungreased 9-inch-by-13-inch pan.

Spoon apricot jam over crumb crust and top with reserved crumbs. Bake for 35 minutes. Cool before cutting.

ALEXANDRA HEMMING

TIP *Quick-cooking rolled oats are pre-cooked but not ground or flattened like instant oatmeal. They have more nutritional value.*

Glazed Apple Cookies

PHOTO ON PAGE 119

MAKES:
About 4 dozen.

FREEZEWORTHY:
No. The cookie will become softer and the frosting watery when thawed.

NOTES

Leave out the nuts and you'll have a soft, familiar-tasting cookie that small children will love.

2 cups sifted all-purpose flour
1 teaspoon baking soda
½ teaspoon salt
1 teaspoon cinnamon
1 teaspoon ground cloves
½ teaspoon nutmeg
½ cup shortening
1 cup light brown sugar
1 egg
¼ cup apple juice or milk
1 cup chopped nuts
1 cup chopped raisins
1 cup chopped, unpeeled apples (use sweet apples such as Red Delicious or Gala)

FROSTING:
1¾ cups confectioners' sugar
1½ tablespoons butter or margarine
3½ tablespoons milk or apple juice
Dash of salt
¼ teaspoon maple flavoring

Preheat oven to 400 degrees.

To make the dough, sift flour, baking soda, salt and spices together; set aside.

Cream shortening and brown sugar; beat in the egg. Add sifted dry ingredients alternately with apple juice or milk. Fold in chopped nuts, raisins and apples. Drop by heaping teaspoonsful onto greased cookie sheet about 2 inches apart.

Bake for 10 to 12 minutes, and then remove from cookie sheet.

To make the frosting, cream confectioners' sugar and butter or margarine; add milk or apple juice, salt and maple flavoring. Mix until spreading consistency. Frost cookies while they are warm.

DOROTHY HOLLIDAY

Rosemary Shortbread

PHOTO ON PAGE 114

MAKES:
3 dozen.

FREEZEWORTHY:
Yes, but cool completely first.

NOTES

Fresh rosemary's aromatic earthiness brings a sophisticated flair to these buttery shortbread cookies.

1½ cups (2¼ sticks) unsalted butter, room temperature
⅔ cup sugar
2¾ cups all-purpose flour
¼ teaspoon salt
2 tablespoons finely chopped fresh rosemary

In a medium bowl, cream together the butter and sugar until light and fluffy. Stir in the flour, salt and rosemary until well blended. The dough will be somewhat soft. Cover and refrigerate for 30 minutes. Remove and roll into two 1½-inch logs and refrigerate for at least 2 hours.

Preheat oven to 375 degrees.

Line cookie sheets with parchment paper.

Slice dough ¼-inch thick and place 2 inches apart on cookie sheets. Bake for 8 minutes or until golden at the edges. Cool on wire racks, and then store in an airtight container at room temperature.

TIP ! *Use parchment paper to line cookie sheets. It facilitates even baking, prevents sticking and makes cleanup a snap. (This is my No. 1 tip!)*

German Spice Cookies

PHOTO ON PAGE 119

MAKES: 2 to 3 dozen, depending on shape.

FREEZEWORTHY: Yes, but cool completely first.

NOTES

Reader Jean Venturino says this recipe was handed down from her German mother, who called the cookies "Spekuchen." Our research didn't turn up any German cookies by that name, but many recipes call for similar ingredients, including Zimtkekse, a cinnamon cookie. Also, Venturino's cookies are similar to Speculaas, a cookie of Dutch origin made in wooden molds, often in the shape of a windmill. Similar cookies were made in Germany.

2 to 3 cups all-purpose flour
2 teaspoons cinnamon
⅓ teaspoon nutmeg
⅓ teaspoon ground cloves
1 cup (2 sticks) unsalted butter, room temperature
1 cup dark brown sugar
2 tablespoons milk
¼ teaspoon baking soda

CINNAMON SUGAR:
¼ cup granulated sugar
½ teaspoon cinnamon

Sift 2 cups of the flour with the spices. Set aside.

Cream butter. Add sugar and mix well. Add milk, then sifted mixture plus enough additional flour to make a firm dough. Knead dough well to be sure all ingredients are incorporated. Divide dough into two parts, wrap tightly and refrigerate at least overnight. (It will keep up to 2 weeks.)

Preheat oven to 375 degrees.

Dust flour onto pastry cloth or wax paper and roll out dough to about ⅛-inch thickness. Cut into desired shapes.

Combine sugar and cinnamon. Sprinkle over unbaked cookies. Place on ungreased cookie sheets and bake until light brown around the edges, 10 to 15 minutes. Remove to racks and cool before storing. (The more thinly the cookies are rolled, the more easily they burn, so watch carefully the last 3 or 4 minutes.)

JEAN VENTURINO

White Chocolate Macaroons

PHOTO ON PAGE 117

MAKES: 2½ dozen.

FREEZEWORTHY: Yes, but cool completely first.

NOTES

If you can't find white chocolate chunk refrigerated cookie dough, use sugar cookie dough and add white chocolate chips.

1 (18-ounce) package refrigerated white chocolate chunk cookie dough, such as Pillsbury's
2¼ cups shredded coconut
2 teaspoons vanilla
½ teaspoon coconut extract

Preheat oven to 350 degrees.

Lightly grease cookie sheets or line with parchment paper.

Break up the cookie dough in a large bowl. Add all remaining ingredients and mix well. Drop dough by teaspoonful onto cookie sheets.

Bake for 10 to 12 minutes or until golden brown. Cool 2 minutes. Remove from cookie sheets.

CARMEN HUNTER

TIP *Refrigerated dough can be the base for other cookies. Place the dough in a bowl and stir in dried cranberries or cherries, chocolate chips or shredded coconut to make the cookie your own. Bake tablespoons of dough like you would chocolate chip cookies.*

Frosted Date Drops

PHOTO ON PAGE 115

MAKES:
2 to 3 dozen.

FREEZEWORTHY:
No. The soft cookie will become softer and fall apart.

NOTES

This frosted cookie option is delicious served with a cup of tea.

1 cup chopped dates
½ cup water
½ cup (1 stick) butter, room temperature
½ cup brown sugar
1 egg
½ teaspoon vanilla
¼ cup milk
1½ cups all-purpose flour
½ teaspoon salt
½ teaspoon baking powder
¼ teaspoon baking soda
½ cup nuts, chopped

FROSTING:
3 tablespoons butter, room temperature
1½ cups sifted confectioners' sugar
Reserved date mixture
½ teaspoon vanilla
Milk (enough to make mixture spreadable)
Colored sugars

Preheat oven to 375 degrees.

To make the cookies, bring dates and water to boil in a 1-quart saucepan. Lower heat and simmer 5 minutes. Set aside to cool. Reserve 2 tablespoons of the mixture for the frosting.

Beat together cookie ingredients except the nuts until thoroughly blended. Stir in the nuts.

Drop by teaspoonsful onto greased cookie sheet and bake for 10 minutes. Cool.

To make frosting, mix together all ingredients until smooth. Frost cookies and then sprinkle with colored sugars.

SUZANNE ZITZKE

Potato Chip Pecan Crunch Cookies

PHOTO ON PAGE 118

MAKES: 4 dozen.

FREEZEWORTHY: Yes, but cool completely first.

Don't tell anyone there are crushed potato chips in the mix so that all they will care about is the buttery goodness.

1 cup (2 sticks) unsalted butter, room temperature
½ cup sugar plus extra for topping
1 teaspoon vanilla
½ cup crushed potato chips
½ cup chopped pecans
2 cups sifted all-purpose flour

Preheat oven to 350 degrees.

Cream butter, ½ cup of the sugar and vanilla. Stir in potato chips, nuts and flour. Form dough into small balls, using 1 tablespoon dough for each.

Place on ungreased cookie sheets. Press balls flat with bottom of a tumbler dipped in sugar.

Bake for 16 to 18 minutes, until lightly browned.

HELEN GROSS, DOLORES CORNEAU AND CAROL SWANSON

NOTES

Frosted Cashew Cookies

PHOTO ON PAGE 119

MAKES:
5 dozen.

FREEZEWORTHY:
No. The cookie will become softer and the icing won't hold up when thawed.

NOTES

Here is a cookie fit to serve for afternoon tea, bunco or bridge.

½ cup (1 stick) unsalted butter, room temperature
1 cup brown sugar
1 egg
½ teaspoon vanilla
2 cups all-purpose flour
¾ teaspoon baking powder
¾ teaspoon baking soda
1 teaspoon salt
⅓ cup sour cream
1 cup cashew nuts, chopped

FROSTING:
½ cup (1 stick) unsalted butter
3 tablespoons cream
½ teaspoon vanilla
2 cups confectioners' sugar, sifted

Preheat oven to 400 degrees.

To make the dough, cream butter and brown sugar; beat in egg and vanilla. Combine dry ingredients in a medium bowl; add alternately with sour cream. Fold in chopped cashews.

Drop by teaspoonsful onto baking sheet and bake for 10 minutes. Let cool.

To make the frosting, lightly brown butter in a skillet over medium-high heat; remove from heat. Pour melted, browned butter into a mixing bowl and add remaining ingredients. Stir until well mixed and spreadable. Spread on cooled cookies.

PHYLLIS HER

Butter Brickle & Pecan Cookies

PHOTO ON PAGE 116

MAKES:
4 dozen.

FREEZEWORTHY:
Yes, but cool completely first.

Make two batches, one for the cookie jar and the other for the freezer.

2 cups (4 sticks) unsalted butter
1 teaspoon vanilla
4 cups all-purpose flour
2 cups confectioners' sugar
1 bag Heath English Toffee Bits®
2 cups chopped pecans

Preheat oven to 375 degrees.

Melt butter in microwave or double boiler; stir in vanilla and cool completely.

Combine flour and sugar in a large bowl. Stir in butter mixture; add toffee bits and chopped pecans (mixture will be crumbly). Shape into 1-inch balls and place 2 inches apart on ungreased baking sheets. Flatten slightly.

Bake for 12 minutes, or until edges begin to brown.

BARBARA LOVE AND RACHEL LITTLE

NOTES

TIP *Butter can be easily melted in the microwave oven. Put it in a microwave-safe bowl and heat on high in 30-second intervals. A cup will melt in just over 90 seconds.*

Oatmeal Gingersnaps

PHOTO ON PAGE 118

MAKES:
4 dozen.

FREEZEWORTHY:
Yes, but cool completely first.

NOTES

This hearty gingersnap is bulked up with oatmeal. A handful of golden raisins will add interest.

1 cup packed light brown sugar
¾ cup shortening
1 egg
¼ cup light Karo® syrup
1½ cups all-purpose flour
1 cup old-fashioned or quick-cooking oats, uncooked (not instant)
2 teaspoons baking soda
2 teaspoons ground ginger
1 teaspoon ground cinnamon
¼ teaspoon salt
½ cup or more granulated sugar

Combine brown sugar and shortening; beat until creamy. Stir in egg and Karo® syrup.

Add flour, oats, baking soda, ginger, cinnamon and salt to the creamed mixture and mix well. Chill dough for 1 hour.

Preheat oven to 350 degrees.

Sprinkle granulated sugar on a plate and spread it out.

Roll spoonfuls of dough into 1-inch balls, then drop balls into sugar on the plate and roll around to cover.

Place sugared dough balls on a lightly greased cookie sheet 2 inches apart. Bake 8 to 10 minutes or until lightly browned. Let stand 3 minutes before removing to racks to cool.

TOMMY SIMMONS, FOOD EDITOR,
THE ADVOCATE, BATON ROUGE, LA.

Macadamia Snowballs

PHOTO ON PAGE 117

MAKES:
4 dozen.

FREEZEWORTHY:
Yes, but cool completely first.

NOTES

The salty crunch of macadamia nuts brings these sweet snowballs to life. The oats give them a sturdy earthiness and a bit more fiber.

1 cup (2 sticks) unsalted butter, room temperature
½ cup sifted confectioners' sugar
1 teaspoon vanilla
2 cups all-purpose flour
¾ cup quick-cooking oats, uncooked (not instant)
1 (3½-ounce) jar macadamia nuts, chopped
Confectioners' sugar

Preheat oven to 375 degrees.

Beat butter at medium speed with an electric mixer until soft and creamy; gradually add confectioners' sugar, beating well after each addition. Add vanilla and flour, mixing well. Stir in oats and chopped nuts.

Shape dough into 1-inch balls. Place on ungreased cookie sheet. Bake for 12 minutes. Remove from pan. Roll balls in confectioners' sugar and cool on wire racks.

PAT AREND

TIP *Have two sets of measuring cups and spoons so you don't have to keep washing. Better yet, get one set of measuring cups for wet ingredients (a glass or plastic pitcher-like vessel that measures at least 2 cups) and one set for dry ingredients (graduated nesting cups with handles).*

Chubby Hubby Cookies

PHOTO ON PAGE 119

MAKES: 3½ dozen.

FREEZEWORTHY: Yes, but cool completely first.

Take these cookies out of the oven while still soft. They will firm as they cool and the chocolate and peanut butter chips stay intact.

1 cup (2 sticks) unsalted butter, room temperature
½ cup granulated sugar
½ cup light brown sugar, firmly packed
1 large egg
1 tablespoon vanilla
2 cups all-purpose flour
1½ teaspoons baking soda
Pinch of salt
1 cup semisweet chocolate chips
1 cup peanut butter chips
½ cup salted peanuts
1 cup crushed pretzels

Preheat oven to 350 degrees.

Cream butter and sugars in a large bowl until light and fluffy. Beat in egg and vanilla. Combine flour, baking soda and salt in a medium bowl. Blend contents of that bowl into creamed mixture. Stir in chocolate and peanut butter chips, peanuts and pretzels.

Drop heaping tablespoons of the dough about 2 inches apart onto ungreased cookie sheet. Bake 10 to 13 minutes, or until edges are lightly brown and centers are still soft. Do not over bake.

Cool one minute on cookie sheet, and then cool completely on wire racks. Store in tightly covered container.

SHARON CHAMBERLAIN

NOTES

Oatmeal Bourbon Cookies

PHOTO ON PAGE 116

MAKES:
4 dozen.

FREEZEWORTHY:
Yes, but cool completely first.

These cookies will appear "not quite done" when you take them out of the oven, but they will continue cooking on the baking sheet.

1 cup (2 sticks) unsalted butter, room temperature
½ cup packed light brown sugar
1 egg
¼ cup water
1 (18-ounce) package yellow cake mix
3 tablespoons bourbon
3 cups quick-cooking rolled oats (not instant)
1 cup nuts, chopped

Preheat oven to 350 degrees.

Cream butter and sugar in mixer; add egg, water and half package of dry cake mix, blending thoroughly. Stir in remaining cake mix, bourbon, oats and nuts. Drop dough by teaspoonful onto ungreased baking sheet about 2 inches apart. Bake exactly 10 minutes. Do not over bake. Cool slightly and remove from baking sheet.

SHARON W. THOMPSON

NOTES

TIP *When a recipe doesn't specify light or dark brown sugar, go with light. The additional molasses in dark brown sugar might make your cookies darker than you'd like.*

Buffalo Cookies

PHOTO ON PAGE 117

MAKES:
4 to 5 dozen.

FREEZEWORTHY:
Yes, but cool completely first.

NOTES

Another name for this cookie could be Everything but the Kitchen Sink. They might even be hearty enough to stand in for dinner. At 15 minutes, these are very crispy cookies. We like the results at 13 minutes.

1 cup (2 sticks) unsalted butter, melted
½ cup sugar
1 cup brown sugar, firmly packed
1 teaspoon vanilla
2 eggs
1½ cups all-purpose flour
1 teaspoon cinnamon
1 teaspoon baking soda
2 cups old-fashioned or quick-cooking rolled oats, uncooked (not instant)
1 cup crushed cornflakes (or granola or Rice Krispies®)
1 cup semisweet chocolate pieces
½ cup pecans
½ cup coconut flakes

Preheat oven to 350 degrees.

Combine butter, sugars and vanilla; beat until blended. Add eggs and beat until fully incorporated. Gradually add flour, cinnamon and baking soda. Stir in oats, cornflakes, chocolate, pecans and coconut. Dough will be thick.

Using an ice cream scoop (or about ¼ cup per cookie), place balls of dough on a greased cookie sheet, about 3 inches apart. Bake 13 to 15 minutes. Do not over bake.

Let cool on wire racks before putting them into a container.

ANDI BLOUNT

Auntie's Gingersnaps

PHOTO ON PAGE 114

MAKES:
About 5 dozen.

FREEZEWORTHY:
Yes, but cool completely first.

NOTES

These cookies turn out perfectly every time. The shape, the flavor and the ease of preparation make this recipe one of my all-time favorites.

2 cups sugar plus additional sugar for rolling
1½ cups shortening
2 eggs
½ cup molasses
4 cups all-purpose flour
1 teaspoon salt
4 teaspoons baking soda
2 teaspoons cinnamon
2 teaspoons ginger
¾ teaspoon cloves

Preheat oven to 350 degrees.

Cream the 2 cups of sugar and shortening together. Add eggs and molasses, and mix well. Mix in remaining dry ingredients until stiff dough forms.

Form into balls the size of walnuts. Roll balls in granulated sugar. Place 1 inch apart on greased baking sheet. Bake for about 10 minutes.

ELEANOR BERNAT

TIP ***Lightly oil the cup before measuring syrup, honey, molasses and other sticky ingredients and the ingredient will pour out without sticking and you'll get the full measure into your dough.***

No Ordinary Oatmeal Cookies

PHOTO ON PAGE 117

MAKES:
About 3 dozen.

FREEZEWORTHY:
Yes, but cool completely first.

NOTES

Dried apricots and white chocolate chips give oatmeal cookies a boost out of the ordinary.

1 cup all-purpose flour
1 cup granulated sugar, divided use
½ cup light brown sugar, firmly packed
½ teaspoon baking powder
½ teaspoon baking soda
¼ teaspoon salt
½ cup shortening
1 egg
½ teaspoon vanilla
¾ cup quick-cooking rolled oats
¼ cup finely chopped walnuts
¼ cup dried apricots, snipped into small pieces
½ cup white chocolate chips

Preheat oven to 375 degrees.

Stir together in a large bowl, the flour, ½ cup granulated sugar, brown sugar, baking powder, baking soda and salt; set aside. In a separate bowl, combine shortening, egg and vanilla; beat well. Mix in dry ingredients, and then stir in oats, walnuts, apricots and white chocolate chips. Form into small balls.

Put remaining granulated sugar into shallow bowl. Dip tops of cookies into sugar and place on ungreased cookie sheets, about 1 inch apart. Bake for 10 to 12 minutes or until lightly browned. Cool on racks, then store in airtight containers.

KATHY HOCKER AND VICKY ANDERSON

Lemon Coconut Snaps

PHOTO ON PAGE 119

MAKES:
7 dozen.

FREEZEWORTHY:
Yes, but cool completely first.

NOTES

Sweetened coconut pairs nicely with the refreshing pucker of lemon in this sturdy cookie.

1 cup (2 sticks) unsalted butter, room temperature
1 cup sugar
1 egg
2 tablespoons lemon juice
¼ teaspoon lemon extract
2½ cups all-purpose flour
½ teaspoon salt
½ teaspoon baking soda
1 (3½-ounce) can flaked coconut, about 1⅓ cups
Candied cherries, halved (optional)

Preheat oven to 375 degrees.

Cream the butter and sugar until light and fluffy. Add egg, lemon juice and extract; beat well. Stir together flour, salt and baking soda in a medium mixing bowl. Add to creamed mixture; mix well.

Shape into 1-inch balls; roll in coconut and place on ungreased cookie sheet. Flatten with bottom of glass. Top with candied cherry half, if using.

Bake for 10 to 12 minutes. Remove from cookie sheet immediately.

GAIL SLOAN

Key Lime Coolers

PHOTO ON PAGE 114

MAKES:
4 to 5 dozen.

FREEZEWORTHY:
Yes, but you might want to dust them again with confectioners' sugar before serving.

NOTES

For sparkle, add 2 tablespoons of white edible glitter to the confectioners' sugar.

¾ cup (1½ sticks) unsalted butter
¾ cup granulated sugar
½ teaspoon salt
1 teaspoon baking powder
4 tablespoons Key lime juice
3 teaspoons Key lime zest
1 large egg
2½ cups unbleached, all-purpose flour
¼ cup macadamia nuts, chopped (optional)
Confectioners' sugar to dust

Preheat oven to 350 degrees; set oven rack in top third of oven.

Beat together butter, sugar, salt and baking powder in a medium mixing bowl, until well blended. Beat in lime juice, zest and egg. Blend in the flour thoroughly (dough will be rather stiff). If using macadamia nuts, incorporate now. Roll the dough into 1-inch balls and place them on a lightly greased or parchment-lined baking sheet.

Bake for 12 to 16 minutes (just until the cookies are browned on the bottom; they'll still be white on top). Remove from oven; cool on the pan for a few minutes. While still slightly warm, roll in confectioners' sugar or gently shake in a bag of the sugar. Allow cookies to cool completely on wire rack, then coat with sugar again.

B BUCKBERRY

Honey-Roasted Peanut Crisps

PHOTO ON PAGE 115

MAKES:
About 4 dozen.

FREEZEWORTHY:
Yes, but cool completely first.

NOTES

I love the crunch and flavor of honey-roasted peanuts in these cookies. It's a simple addition that makes a world of difference.

1 cup brown sugar, firmly packed
½ cup (1 stick) unsalted butter, room temperature
½ cup shortening
1 teaspoon vanilla
1 egg
2 cups all-purpose flour
2 cups honey-roasted peanuts
½ teaspoon baking powder
¼ teaspoon salt
Granulated sugar

Preheat oven to 375 degrees.

Mix brown sugar, butter, shortening, vanilla and egg in large bowl. Stir in flour, peanuts, baking powder and salt. Mix well.

Drop dough by rounded tablespoonsful about 2 inches apart onto ungreased cookie sheet. Flatten with greased bottom of glass dipped in granulated sugar.

Bake 9 to 10 minutes or until golden brown. Cool slightly; remove from cookie sheet. Cool on wire rack.

SHIRLEY HAWKINS

TIP ***Use unsalted nuts in recipes; save the salted versions for snacking and as accompaniments with cocktails.***

Moon Cookies

PHOTO ON PAGE 115

MAKES:
3 dozen.

FREEZEWORTHY:
Yes, but cool completely first.

NOTES

Cashews and white chocolate combine for an unusual, but delicious, cookie. Look for oatmeal flour at health food stores, or grind oatmeal yourself in a food processor.

1 cup (2 sticks) unsalted butter, room temperature
1 cup light brown sugar
1 cup sugar
2 large eggs
1 teaspoon vanilla
2 cups all-purpose flour
2½ cups oatmeal flour
¼ teaspoon salt
1 teaspoon baking soda
1 teaspoon baking powder
12 ounces white chocolate morsels
4 ounces white chocolate baking squares, sliced into ⅛-inch slices
1½ cups split cashews

Preheat oven to 375 degrees.

Cream the butter with both sugars. Mix in eggs and vanilla. Add flour and mix well, then add oatmeal flour, salt, baking soda and baking power. Using a large spoon, mix in white chocolate morsels and baking square slices.

Add split cashews (The splits should look like quarter moons). Mix well. Roll into 1-inch balls and place on cookie sheet 2 inches apart. Bake for 10 minutes. If you bake them longer, they will be hard.

JOEY VALDEZ

Coconut Krispies Drops

PHOTO ON PAGE 114

MAKES:
3 to 4 dozen.

FREEZEWORTHY:
No. The drops will lose the snap of the cereal and can get gummy.

NOTES

These are similar to Rice Krispies® Treats but not as sweet or sticky. Forming balls is easier if you wet hands or spritz with nonstick spray.

2 eggs
1 cup sugar
1½ cups (8-ounce) package chopped dates
½ cup chopped walnuts
1 teaspoon vanilla
Pinch of salt
2 cups Rice Krispies®
1 to 2 cups toasted coconut (see note)

Combine eggs and sugar in a 3-quart saucepan until well mixed. Place pan over medium-low heat, stirring constantly for 10 minutes.

Add dates, walnuts, vanilla, salt and Rice Krispies® and then remove from heat. Cool enough to shape into 1-inch balls. Roll in toasted coconut.

NOTE: To toast shredded coconut, place on a baking sheet. Bake in a preheated 350 degree oven, stirring every 30 seconds, until the coconut is dry and light brown with some white shreds. The process takes 2 to 4 minutes.

MARGE V. BERGERON

TIP ! ***Substitute the chopped dates in this recipe with dried cherries or cranberries, or even dried tropical fruits such as pineapple or mango.***

Coconut Oatmeal Cookies

PHOTO ON PAGE 114

MAKES:
About 45 cookies.

FREEZEWORTHY:
Yes, but cool completely first.

NOTES

Here's a sweet twist on traditional oatmeal cookies. Add ⅔ cup dried fruit such as raisins, cranberries or cherries to spike flavor and interest.

1½ cups all-purpose flour
1 teaspoon cinnamon
1 teaspoon baking soda
1 teaspoon salt
¼ teaspoon freshly grated or ground nutmeg
1 cup (2 sticks) unsalted butter, room temperature
¾ cup packed light brown sugar
½ cup sugar
1 large egg
1 teaspoon vanilla
1¾ cups old-fashioned rolled oats
1¼ cups sweetened flaked coconut

Preheat oven to 375 degrees; set oven rack in middle of oven.

Sift together flour, cinnamon, baking soda, salt and nutmeg into a small bowl. Set aside. Beat together butter and sugars with an electric mixer until light and fluffy. Beat in egg and vanilla, and then stir in flour mixture, oats and coconut until combined well.

Drop rounded tablespoons or a No. 40 ice cream scoop of dough 3 inches apart on ungreased cookie sheets and gently flatten mounds into 3-inch rounds. Bake cookies until golden, 10 to 12 minutes. Cool cookies on cookie sheets 1 minute, and then cool completely on a rack.

KATHRYN WILSON

Toffee Crisps

PHOTO ON PAGE 119

MAKES: 6 dozen.

FREEZEWORTHY: Yes, but cool completely first.

NOTES

If you can't find toffee chips, start hammering away at Heath® bars.

1 cup sugar
½ cup packed brown sugar
½ cup (1 stick) unsalted butter, room temperature
1 teaspoon vanilla
2 eggs
2¼ cups all-purpose flour
1 teaspoon baking powder
½ teaspoon baking soda
½ teaspoon salt
1 cup almond brickle or toffee chips

Preheat oven to 350 degrees.

Cream the sugars and butter in a mixing bowl until light and fluffy. Add the vanilla and eggs; beat well.

In a separate bowl, mix flour, baking powder, baking soda and salt. Incorporate into the wet mixture. Stir in the almond brickle or toffee chips.

Drop by rounded teaspoonsful 2 inches apart on to a cookie sheet sprayed with non-stick cooking spray. Bake for 8 to 12 minutes or until light golden brown. Remove from cookie sheets immediately and cool on wire racks.

SHIRLEY BUTTACAVOLI

TIP ❗ ***Cool cookies on wire racks rather than on baking sheets or plates. Cookies cooled on solid surfaces get mushy on the bottom and those left to cool on hot baking sheets lose moisture.***

Honey Cookies

PHOTO ON PAGE 116

MAKES:
3 dozen.

FREEZEWORTHY:
Yes, but cool completely first.

NOTES

Celebrate the work of honey bees with these deliciously different cookies.

2½ cups all-purpose flour
1 teaspoon baking soda
1 teaspoon cinnamon
1 teaspoon ground coriander
½ teaspoon salt
½ cup (1 stick) unsalted butter, room temperature
½ cup brown sugar, packed
¾ cup honey
1 egg
1 teaspoon vanilla
½ cup raisins
¾ cup walnuts, chopped

Preheat oven to 350 degrees.

Sift flour in a large mixing bowl with baking soda, cinnamon, coriander and salt. In separate bowl, cream together butter, brown sugar, honey, egg and vanilla. Add flour mixture to butter mixture, stirring until well combined. Stir in raisins and walnuts.

Drop batter by teaspoonsful on to greased cookie sheets or cookie sheets lined with parchment paper.

Bake for 10 minutes.

ADRIENNE S. ROBERTS

Toffee Squares

PHOTO ON PAGE 115

MAKES: About 54 cookies.

FREEZEWORTHY: Yes, but cool completely first.

NOTES

Take these cookies to a potluck dessert party or keep them for yourself. They are impressive but simple to make at the same time.

1 cup (2 sticks) unsalted butter or margarine, room temperature
1 cup packed light brown sugar
1 egg yolk
1 teaspoon vanilla
2 cups all-purpose flour
1 cup (6 ounces) semisweet chocolate pieces
1 cup chopped walnuts

Preheat oven to 350 degrees.

Line a 15-inch-by-10-inch jelly-roll pan with foil. Beat together in a medium bowl, butter or margarine, brown sugar, egg yolk and vanilla until light and fluffy. Add flour in batches, beating after each addition until well blended. Spread mixture in the foil-lined pan. Bake 15 to 18 minutes or until golden.

Sprinkle chocolate pieces evenly over cookie surface. Bake 2 to 3 minutes or until chocolate melts. Remove from oven and let stand 1 minute. With a knife, spread melted chocolate evenly over top.

Sprinkle with walnuts. Cut into squares while warm; cool in pan. Store in refrigerator, if desired.

NATALIE HAUGHTON, FOOD EDITOR,
LOS ANGELES DAILY NEWS

TIP *Always buy pure vanilla extract rather than imitation flavoring for best results. If you're taking the time to make cookies from scratch, you'll want to make sure the ingredients are top-notch.*

Lemon Nutmeg Meltaways

PHOTO ON PAGE 115

MAKES:
2 dozen.

FREEZEWORTHY:
Yes, but cool completely first.

NOTES

Don't skimp on the grated lemon peel because that's what gives these cookies their pucker power.

1 cup sifted cake flour
½ cup cornstarch
¼ teaspoon salt
½ teaspoon ground nutmeg
10 tablespoons (1 stick plus 2 tablespoons) unsalted butter, room temperature
½ cup confectioners' sugar plus a little extra
2 teaspoons grated lemon rind

Preheat oven to 350 degrees.

Sift cake flour, cornstarch, salt and nutmeg onto wax paper. Set aside.

Beat butter, the ½ cup of confectioners' sugar and lemon rind with electric mixer until light and fluffy. Add sifted dry ingredients to butter mixture, beating on low speed until mixture is smooth.

Roll teaspoons of the dough into balls; place on ungreased cookie sheet. Flatten slightly to 1¼-inch circles with bottom of glass dipped in extra confectioners' sugar.

Bake for 15 minutes, or until cookies have turned pale brown on edges. When cool, pack into airtight containers and store up to one week.

LOLA KUSLANSKY

Cream Cheese Roll-Ups

PHOTO ON PAGE 116

MAKES:
5 to 6 dozen.

FREEZEWORTHY:
No. The cookies will become too soft and fall apart when thawed.

NOTES

This is not a super-sweet cookie, which makes it a nice addition to a plate of richer treats. Use a ravioli wheel to give the cookies a decorative edge.

1 cup (2 sticks) unsalted butter, room temperature
8 ounces cream cheese
2 cups sifted all-purpose flour
¼ teaspoon salt
Confectioners' sugar
Pitted dates, candied cherries or pecan halves

Cream together butter and cream cheese. Blend in flour and salt. Chill for several hours or until dough is firm enough to roll.

Preheat oven to 375 degrees.

Roll dough to ⅛-inch thickness, using dusting of flour to prevent dough from sticking to surface and rolling pin. Sprinkle with confectioners' sugar.

Cut into 1-inch-by-3-inch strips with pastry wheel. Put a date, cherry or pecan half in center of each strip and roll up. Put the folded side down on ungreased cookie sheet.

Bake for 15 minutes, until lightly brown. Cool slightly and then sprinkle with confectioners' sugar.

TONI REINWALD

TIP *Always use unsalted butter, and if a recipe calls for margarine, make sure it's in stick form rather than from a tub. Do not use margarine that's less than 60 percent fat; it has more water in it and will make cookies very soft and perhaps spread more than they should in the oven.*

Nut-Ribbon Strips

PHOTO ON PAGE 118

MAKES:
5 dozen.

FREEZEWORTHY:
Yes, but cool completely first. Sprinkle with confectioners' sugar again after thawing.

NOTES

Use whatever chopped nuts you like for these cookies that are cut and baked in strips. I prefer pecans, but toasted walnuts work just as well.

1 cup (2 sticks) unsalted butter, room temperature
½ cup sugar
1 teaspoon almond extract
1 egg
2 cups all-purpose flour
2 teaspoons baking powder
¼ teaspoon salt
½ cup chopped nuts
Confectioners' sugar

Cream butter, sugar and almond extract. Add egg and beat well. Add flour, baking powder and salt; beat well until completely combined. Chill dough 45 minutes.

Preheat oven to 350 degrees.

On floured board, roll dough into rectangle about ¼-inch thick. Sprinkle with chopped nuts. Press in lightly with rolling pin. Cut dough into strips, about 1-inch wide and 2½-inches long. Place strips on greased cookie sheet and press tops with a fork.

Bake for 10 to 12 minutes. Remove and cool. Dust with confectioners' sugar.

CAROL J. HOOVER

CHAPTER 2

SHARING

GIFTS FROM THE KITCHEN FOR SPECIAL OCCASIONS AND JUST BECAUSE

A gift of homemade cookies is a present from the heart. The new neighbors will appreciate a plate of baked goods to welcome them to their home. So will a friend who has been struggling or another who is celebrating a promotion at work. What about the family with a new baby, a friend who is turning 30 or a recent graduate? Cookies, cookies, cookies.

There are many occasions to bake for family and friends, and sometimes you don't even need a reason to share a gift from the kitchen. How nice to split a batch with co-workers or even the dedicated person who delivers your mail.

The recipes in this chapter bring something special to homemade treats that make them perfect for giving. Look through the recipes for inexpensive ideas to present them.

SHARING ! COOKIES

Tipsies

PHOTO ON PAGE 125

MAKES:
About 4 dozen.

FREEZEWORTHY:
Yes, after they've "ripened."

Tipsies can be kept in the refrigerator in an air-tight container for a long time (if you can keep yourself from nibbling them away).

1 (6-ounce) package semisweet chocolate chips
1 tablespoon light corn syrup
⅓ cup bourbon
2½ cups (7½-ounce package) finely crushed vanilla wafers
1 cup finely chopped nuts
½ cup confectioners' sugar

Melt chocolate chips in top of a double boiler. Add corn syrup and bourbon. Mix well. Combine crushed vanilla wafers and nuts in large bowl. Pour chocolate mixture over dry ingredients and mix well. Let stand 30 minutes.

Shape into 1-inch balls and roll in confectioners' sugar. Store in tightly closed container and let ripen several days before needed.

GLORIA MADLINGER

NOTES

TIP *Decorative plates: All through the year, collect inexpensive plates to use for cookies you will be giving away. They are easy to find on clearance, especially after the holidays, but dedicated shoppers will find cut-rate plates and platters year 'round. Garage sales are also good sources. Besides using them as a beautiful way to present cookies, the plate is part of the offering.*

Peanut Butter Sandwich Cookies

PHOTO ON PAGE 125

MAKES:
About 3 dozen.

FREEZEWORTHY:
Not recommended.

NOTES

I should call these "Jenny's Favorites" because my friend's daughter, Jenny, requests them all the time. She swears she doesn't like peanut butter cookies! These are always a hit with her and everyone else who tastes them. Thanks to Peggy Katalinich, food editor of Family Circle, for sharing them.

COOKIE:

1½ cups all-purpose flour
¾ teaspoon baking soda
¼ teaspoon salt
½ cup (1 stick) unsalted butter, room temperature
½ cup creamy peanut butter, room temperature
1 cup granulated sugar
1 large egg

FILLING:

¾ cup peanut butter
¼ cup confectioners' sugar

GLAZE:

1 cup semisweet chocolate chips
4 teaspoons vegetable oil

Preheat oven to 350 degrees.

To make the cookies, combine flour, baking soda and salt in a medium bowl. Set aside. Beat together in a large bowl, butter, peanut butter, sugar and egg until smooth. Beat in flour mixture with an electric mixer set on low.

For each cookie, roll 1 rounded teaspoon of the dough into a 1-inch ball. Place balls 2 inches apart on ungreased baking sheets.

Bake for 10 minutes until puffed. Let stand 2 minutes on sheet. Remove cookies to rack; cool.

To make the filling, mix together peanut butter and confectioners' sugar. Spread flat side of half the cookies with 1 rounded teaspoon filling; top with remaining cookies.

Refrigerate until firm, about 30 minutes.

To make the glaze, combine chips and oil in small microwave-safe bowl, and then heat at full power for one minute; stir until melted. Dip cookies halfway into chocolate; let excess drain off. Place cookies on waxed paper-lined cookie sheets. Drizzle with remaining chocolate. Refrigerate to set.

PEGGY KATALINICH, FOOD EDITOR,
FAMILY CIRCLE

Pecan Puffs

PHOTO ON PAGE 123

MAKES:
About 2 dozen.

FREEZEWORTHY:
Yes, but they may need another roll in confectioners' sugar after they have thawed.

These nutty, confectioners'-sugar balls are a wonderful gift for a friend who needs a pick-me-up, even when the weather is warm.

½ cup (1 stick) butter, room temperature
2 tablespoons sugar
1 teaspoon vanilla
1 cup all-purpose flour
1 cup pecans, finely chopped
Confectioners' sugar

Preheat oven to 300 degrees.

Cream butter. Add sugar, vanilla, flour and nuts. Roll dough into balls and place on ungreased cookie sheet. Bake for approximately 35 to 45 minutes. Remove from oven. Let cool for 5 minutes. Roll in confectioners' sugar. Let cool again and then roll again in confectioners' sugar.

LOIS JOST

NOTES

TIP *Nuts stored in the shell last longer than those that are not. Shelled nuts should be kept in a cool, dark place but they should be used within a month of purchase. If wrapped well, they'll stay fresh in the freezer for one year.*

Orange Drop Cookies

PHOTO ON PAGE 124

MAKES:
About 4 dozen.

FREEZEWORTHY:
No. The already soft cookie will fall apart and frosting will be watery.

NOTES

There is lots of citrus punch in these delicate cookies. You could experiment by substituting lemon, or maybe Key lime, zest for the orange.

⅔ cup shortening
1½ cups sugar
1 egg
½ cup sour cream
½ cup orange juice
1 teaspoon orange extract
2 tablespoons grated orange rind
2½ cups all-purpose flour
½ teaspoon baking powder
½ teaspoon baking soda
½ teaspoon salt

ICING:
2 cups sifted confectioners' sugar
2 tablespoons unsalted butter, slightly softened (do not melt)
4 tablespoons orange juice
1 teaspoon orange extract
Orange zest for decorating

Heat oven to 400 degrees.

To make the cookies, combine shortening, sugar, egg and sour cream in a mixing bowl. Stir in orange juice, extract and rind.

Whisk together flour, baking powder, baking soda and salt in separate bowl. Stir into orange juice mixture until well combined. Dough will be soft; if too soft to drop, add more flour to reach the desired consistency.

Drop rounded teaspoonsful 2 inches apart on an ungreased baking sheet. Bake 8 to 10 minutes.

To make icing, combine confectioners' sugar and butter and then add orange juice and extract to make frosting spreadable. If more sugar is needed, sift it over the bowl and combine well to prevent lumps.

Frost cookies when they are cool.

JAN NORRIS, FOOD EDITOR,
JANNORRIS.COM

Amaretto Butter Balls

PHOTO ON PAGE 120

MAKES: 24 cookies.

FREEZEWORTHY: Yes, but wait to roll them in confectioners' sugar after they thaw.

Friends with sophisticated tastes will appreciate these spiked morsels.

1 cup (2 sticks) unsalted butter, room temperature
1 cup confectioners' sugar, divided use
2½ cups all-purpose flour
1 teaspoon salt
¼ cup amaretto liqueur
¾ cup finely chopped almonds (optional)

Preheat oven to 350 degrees.

Cream the butter and ½ cup of the confectioners' sugar in a medium-sized mixing bowl until smooth. Stir in the flour and salt until well blended, and then mix in the liqueur. Fold in chopped almonds, if desired. Roll the dough into walnut-size balls. Place the cookies 2 inches apart on the cookie sheet.

Bake for 8 to 10 minutes. Allow cookies to cool on baking sheet for 5 minutes before removing to a wire rack to cool completely. Roll cookies in remaining ½ cup of the confectioners' sugar while they are still warm.

JANET K. KEELER

NOTES

TIP *Beggar's purses: Cut fabric such as velvet, gingham, holiday novelty print or even netting into squares. Put a bag of cookies in the middle, draw up the edges and secure with colorful cloth or gold ribbon. You don't have to sew; just cut the fabric with pinking shears to prevent threads from unraveling. Look for supplies in craft stores.*

Frosted Molasses Squares

PHOTO ON PAGE 122

MAKES:
About 3 dozen.

FREEZEWORTHY:
Not the best candidates for freezing because icing gets gummy.

NOTES

These iced squares offer a taste of the Old South. Nuts and raisins give them the bulk they need to stand-up to the sticky icing.

¼ cup shortening
½ cup sugar
1 egg
½ cup dark molasses
2 cups sifted all-purpose flour
1½ teaspoons baking powder
¼ teaspoon baking soda
¼ teaspoon salt
½ cup milk
½ teaspoon vanilla
½ cup raisins
½ cup nuts, coarsely chopped

FROSTING:
2 tablespoons unsalted butter, softened
1 cup sifted confectioners' sugar
1 tablespoon molasses

Water to thin frosting

Preheat oven to 375 degrees.

To make the squares, cream shortening and sugar. Add egg and molasses; mix well. Combine the flour, baking powder, baking soda and salt; add to shortening mixture alternately with milk, beginning and ending with the flour mixture. Stir in vanilla, raisins and nuts. Bake for 20 to 25 minutes in a well-greased, 10-inch-by-15-inch jelly-roll pan.

While the squares are cooking, make the frosting by combining the butter, confectioners' sugar and molasses in a mixing bowl. Beat well, adding water by the teaspoon until mixture is of a spreadable consistency. Frost the squares while they are still warm.

BONNIE WHITAKER

Peach Streusel Bars

PHOTO ON PAGE 124

MAKES:
16 bars.

FREEZEWORTHY:
No. The filling will become too runny when thawed.

NOTES

No need to wait for summer peaches thanks to jarred preserves.

2 cups all-purpose flour
½ cup firmly packed light brown sugar
1 teaspoon grated lemon zest
¼ teaspoon ground nutmeg
¼ teaspoon salt
¾ cup (1½ sticks) unsalted butter
1 (12-ounce) jar peach preserves

Preheat oven to 375 degrees. Grease 9-inch square pan.

Combine flour, sugar, zest, nutmeg and salt in a large bowl. Cut in butter with a pastry blender until mixture is crumbly. Reserve 1 cup. Pat remaining mixture evenly onto the bottom of the prepared pan.

Spread preserves evenly over dough, leaving ¼-inch border around edge. Sprinkle with reserved flour mixture.

Bake for 40 minutes or until lightly browned. Cool in pan on wire rack. Cut into bite-sized bars. Store for up to one week in air-tight container.

MARION HAUPT

TIP *A jar of whole nutmegs lasts for a quite a long time and the flavor of freshly-ground nutmeg beats the pre-ground versions.*

Coffee Toffee Bars

PHOTO ON PAGE 122

MAKES:
3 dozen.

FREEZEWORTHY:
No.

NOTES

If you use a slightly smaller jelly roll pan than called for, your bars will be more cakelike.

BASE:
1 cup (2 sticks) unsalted butter, room temperature
1 cup brown sugar
1 teaspoon almond extract
1 to 2 tablespoons instant coffee granules
½ teaspoon baking powder
¼ teaspoon salt
2 to 2½ cups sifted all-purpose flour
1 cup semisweet chocolate chips
½ cup chopped almonds

ALMOND GLAZE:
1 tablespoon softened unsalted butter
¾ cup sifted confectioners' sugar
⅛ teaspoon almond extract
1 to 2 tablespoons milk

Preheat oven to 350 degrees.

Cream butter and brown sugar with electric mixer on high speed. Blend in extract, coffee granules, baking powder and salt. Add sifted flour to form a stiff dough. Stir in chocolate chips and almonds.

Press dough into a greased 15-inch-by-10-inch-by-1-inch jelly roll pan. Bake for 20 to 25 minutes.

While dough is cooking, make glaze by mixing butter, confectioners' sugar and almond extract together by hand in medium bowl. Add milk until glaze is spreading consistency.

Glaze warm base before cutting into bars.

LISA KOTHE

Cream Cheese & Basil Cookies

PHOTO ON PAGE 124

MAKES:
About 4½ dozen.

FREEZEWORTHY:
So-so results. This is a soft cookie that will be even softer after freezing.

NOTES

Yes, you read right: basil. When mixed with sweet ingredients, the savory herb adds a sophisticated background note.

1 (8-ounce) package cream cheese, room temperature
¼ cup (½ stick) unsalted butter, room temperature
1 egg yolk
2 teaspoons water or milk
1 (18-ounce) package yellow cake mix
3 teaspoons white vinegar
2 teaspoons finely shredded lemon peel
¼ cup coconut
¼ cup chopped nuts
¼ cup finely chopped fresh basil

Preheat oven to 350 degrees.

Cream the cheese and butter with an electric mixer, about 30 seconds. Beat in egg yolk and water or milk. Beat in as much cake mix as you can using the mixer; finish mixing by hand. Stir in vinegar and lemon peel until just combined; add coconut, nuts and basil. Drop by rounded teaspoonful onto ungreased cookie sheet. Bake for 10 to 12 minutes.

EUNICE PINTA

TIP *Cookie jars: This container makes a gift within a gift. There are many kinds of cookie jars, even ones that talk, available in a wide range of price and design. Make sure, though, that the recipient wants a cookie jar. Otherwise, you might see it at the next garage sale.*

Cherry Chocolate Stripes

PHOTO ON PAGE 121

MAKES:
6 to 7 dozen.

FREEZEWORTHY:
Yes, but cool completely first.

NOTES

They look complicated, these layered cookies, but once you get the technique down, they are a snap. Plus, they are pretty to give and even better to eat.

1 cup (2 sticks) unsalted butter, room temperature
1½ cups sugar
1 egg
1 teaspoon vanilla
¼ teaspoon almond extract
2½ cups all-purpose flour
1½ teaspoons baking powder
½ teaspoon salt
½ cup finely chopped candied cherries, divided
1 ounce unsweetened chocolate, melted
¼ cup chopped almonds

Line bottom and sides of 9-inch loaf pan with aluminum foil.

Beat butter at medium speed with electric mixer until creamy. Gradually beat in sugar. Add egg, vanilla and almond extract; mix well. Combine flour, baking powder and salt in a separate bowl. Gradually add to butter, mixing until well blended. Dough will be stiff.

Divide dough into thirds. Add half the cherries to a third, kneading to blend. Press into bottom of prepared pan. Knead melted chocolate and almonds into another third. Press evenly over cherry layer. Add remaining cherries to remaining third of dough and press evenly over chocolate layer. Cover and refrigerate at least 8 hours. When ready to bake, preheat oven to 350 degrees. Invert pan; remove foil from dough.

Cut dough lengthwise into 3 strips. Cut each strip crosswise into ¼-inch slices. Place 1 inch apart on ungreased baking sheets. Bake 10 to 12 minutes. Cool on racks.

KATHLEEN PURVIS, FOOD EDITOR,
CHARLOTTE (N.C.) OBSERVER

Chewy Pecan Bars

PHOTO ON PAGE 121

MAKES: About 2 dozen.

FREEZEWORTHY: No. These soft bars will fall apart easily after thawing.

NOTES

If you know someone who loves pecan pie, this will be a welcome treat, especially when Thanksgiving is months away.

¼ cup (½ stick) unsalted butter, melted
2 cups brown sugar, packed
⅔ cup all-purpose flour
4 eggs
2 teaspoons vanilla
¼ teaspoon baking soda
¼ teaspoon salt
2 cups chopped pecans
Confectioners' sugar

Preheat oven to 350 degrees.

Pour melted butter into a 9-inch-by-13-inch baking pan; set aside.

In mixing bowl, combine brown sugar, flour, eggs, vanilla, baking soda and salt; mix well. Stir in pecans. Spread over melted butter.

Bake for 30 to 35 minutes.

Remove from oven; immediately dust with confectioners' sugar. Cool before cutting.

RENATE APPLEGATE

TIP *Paint buckets: Clean, empty shiny metal paint buckets purchased at hardware stores are great gift containers. If you've got a lot of cookies to give away, go for the gallon bucket; if not, buy a quart container. Make your own label on a computer or by hand. It's a good project for the kids.*

Butter Pecan Turtle Bars

PHOTO ON PAGE 123

MAKES:
3 to 4 dozen bars.

FREEZEWORTHY:
Yes, but cool completely and cut bars first.

NOTES

These decadent bars are the perfect way to say "thank you" or even "I'm sorry." Any transgression will be forgotten once your caramel-lover takes a bite.

BOTTOM LAYER:
2 cups all-purpose flour
½ cup (1 stick) unsalted butter, room temperature
1 cup light brown sugar, firmly packed
1 cup whole pecan halves

CARAMEL LAYER:
⅔ cup unsalted butter
½ cup light brown sugar, firmly packed
1 cup milk chocolate chips

Preheat oven to 350 degrees.

To make the bottom layer, combine flour, butter and brown sugar in a 3-quart bowl. Mix at medium speed for 2 to 3 minutes, scraping bowl frequently. Pat firmly into ungreased 9-inch-by-13-inch pan. Sprinkle pecan pieces evenly over unbaked crust. Set aside.

To make the caramel layer, combine butter and brown sugar in a heavy 1-quart saucepan. Cook over medium heat, stirring constantly until entire surface of mixture begins to boil. Boil 30 seconds to 1 minute, stirring constantly. Pour over pecans and crust.

Bake near center of the oven for 18 to 22 minutes, until caramel layer is bubbly and crust is lightly browned. Remove from oven. Immediately sprinkle chocolate chips over the top. Allow chips to melt slightly, 2 to 3 minutes. Slightly swirl chips with a spatula as they melt, leaving some whole. Cool completely.

ANN M. EZROW

Best-Ever Brickle

PHOTO ON PAGE 120

MAKES:
About 3 dozen pieces.

FREEZEWORTHY:
No.

NOTES

This hall-of-fame recipe is super simple; and everyone who takes a bite thinks brickle is the best treat they've ever had.

40 saltine crackers
1 cup (2 sticks) unsalted butter
1 cup brown sugar
1 (12-ounce) package chocolate chips
Chopped nuts

Preheat oven to 400 degrees.

Cover baking sheet with foil; make sure the sheet has a lip on it. Place saltine crackers in single layer on foil.

Melt butter and brown sugar in a 1-quart saucepan over medium heat. Bring to full boil and cook 3 minutes, stirring constantly. Remove and pour over crackers. Bake for 5 minutes.

Sprinkle chocolate chips on top. Leave until melted, about 1 minute. Spread the softened chocolate with a spatula and then sprinkle with nuts.

Refrigerate for at least 4 hours. Break into pieces.

Store in airtight container in refrigerator.

JUDITH L. MCVAUGH AND CAROL LATTA MILNER

TIP *Boxes and tins: Decorative tins are available at craft stores and discount outlets for less than $5. Search antique stores for anything interesting on the cheap. White or natural-colored cardboard boxes, embossed with designs or plain, can be spray-painted or decorated by children to create engaging gift containers.*

Cashew Yummies

PHOTO ON PAGE 120

MAKES:
2 dozen.

FREEZEWORTHY:
Yes, but cool completely and cut bars first.

NOTES

A few minutes under the broiler makes the topping for these bars bubbly and brown.

BASE:
½ cup granulated sugar
½ cup brown sugar, packed
2 eggs
1 cup all-purpose flour
½ teaspoon baking powder
¼ teaspoon salt
½ cup chopped salted cashews

TOPPING:
2 tablespoons unsalted butter
⅓ cup chopped cashews
¼ cup brown sugar, packed
1½ tablespoons half-and-half

Preheat oven to 350 degrees.

Grease a 9-inch square pan. Set aside.

To make the base, combine sugar, brown sugar and eggs. Mix well. Stir in flour, baking powder, salt and cashews. Pour batter into prepared pan. Bake for 20 to 25 minutes.

Remove from the oven and turn on the broiler.

To make the topping, melt butter in a 1-quart pan and then remove from source of heat. Add cashews, brown sugar and half-and-half. Mix well.

Immediately spread baked bars with topping. Broil about 12 inches from heat for 1 or 2 minutes, or until bubbly and golden.

MARY WILKINSON

Cornmeal Lemon Cookies

PHOTO ON PAGE 122

MAKES:
About 3½ dozen.

FREEZEWORTHY:
Yes, but cool completely first.

NOTES

This dough is crumbly and dense and you might need to use your hands to mix thoroughly.

1¼ cups sifted all-purpose flour
1 teaspoon baking powder
½ teaspoon salt
½ cup enriched white cornmeal
¾ cup sugar
½ cup shortening
1 egg
Grated rind of 1 lemon
1 teaspoon vanilla
1 tablespoon milk
¼ cup finely chopped walnuts

Preheat oven to 350 degrees.

Sift together the flour, baking powder, salt, cornmeal and sugar in a mixing bowl. Add shortening, egg, lemon rind, vanilla and milk. Beat until smooth, 2 minutes or longer. Shape dough into small balls; dip tops in walnuts. Place about 2 inches apart on ungreased cookie sheets. Bake about 15 minutes. Remove to wire racks to cool.

MRS. G.E. NOBLES

TIP *Follow directions exactly when it comes to sifting dry ingredients. Sometimes the directions call for the flour to be sifted first, then measured, and other recipes call for the opposite. One cup sifted flour will yield a different amount than 1 cup flour, sifted.*

Lemon Raspberry Thumbprints

PHOTO ON PAGE 125

MAKES:
4 dozen.

FREEZEWORTHY:
So-so results.
The jam can get gummy when thawed.

NOTES

This Emeril Lagasse recipe is a twist on the traditional thumbprint cookie and is perfect for people who don't like nuts, which are typical in thumbprints. They are delicate and simply delicious.

½ cup raspberry jam or jelly
1 tablespoon Chambord® or Kirsch
2¼ cups all-purpose flour
1 teaspoon baking powder
¼ teaspoon salt
1 cup (2 sticks) unsalted butter, room temperature
⅔ cup sugar
2 large egg yolks
1 tablespoon finely grated lemon zest
1 tablespoon fresh lemon juice
1 teaspoon pure vanilla

Preheat oven to 350 degrees. Lightly butter two large baking sheets.

Whisk together the jam and the Chambord® or Kirsch in a small bowl. Set aside. Combine the flour, baking powder, and salt in a medium mixing bowl, blending well. Set aside.

Beat together the butter and sugar in a large bowl using an electric mixer, until light and creamy. Beat in the egg yolks, lemon zest, lemon juice and vanilla. Add the flour mixture in 2 additions and beat just until moist clumps form. Gather the dough together into a ball.

Pinch off the dough to form 1-inch balls. Place on the prepared baking sheets, spacing 1 inch apart. Use your floured index finger or a ½ teaspoon measuring spoon to create depressions in the center of each ball. Fill each indentation with ½ teaspoon of the jam mixture. Bake until golden brown, about 20 minutes. Transfer the cookies to wire racks to cool completely.

Cookies D'Italia

PHOTO ON PAGE 121

MAKES:
About 3 dozen.

FREEZEWORTHY:
Yes, but cool completely first.

NOTES

These slice-and-bakes are a gift that will impress a very special friend.

8 ounces hazelnuts
1 cup sugar
¾ cup all-purpose flour
2 teaspoons cinnamon
2 tablespoons fresh orange zest
1 teaspoon baking powder
1½ tablespoons rum
4 ounces sweet chocolate, melted
1 egg, beaten

Heat nuts in a dry skillet over medium heat. When slightly brown and aromatic, remove from pan. Cool and then chop. Set aside.

To make the dough, mix sugar, flour, cinnamon, zest and baking powder in a large bowl. Add rum, chocolate and beaten egg, blending (or kneading) well, as dough is stiff.

Add toasted nuts. Form into rolls about 1¾ inches in diameter. Wrap and refrigerate. Dough must be chilled several hours or overnight.

About 10 minutes before baking, preheat oven to 350 degrees.

Cut rolls into ½-inch slices and bake on ungreased cookie sheets for 10 minutes. Cookies are light, dry and chewy.

LISA BAZZANELLA SMITH

TIP *To chill cookie dough quickly, divide it into smaller portions and shape it into discs. Cover with plastic wrap and place in the refrigerator.*

Hazelnut Crinkle Cookies

PHOTO ON PAGE 122

MAKES:
About 2 dozen.

FREEZEWORTHY:
Yes, but cool completely first.

NOTES

A jar of chocolate hazelnut spread lends a distinctive flavor to the cookies that will crack and crinkle in the oven.

½ cup chopped hazelnuts
3 cups all-purpose flour
2 teaspoons baking powder
½ teaspoon salt
1 (11-ounce) jar chocolate hazelnut spread (Nutella®)
¼ cup shortening
1½ cups sugar
1 teaspoon vanilla
2 eggs
⅓ cup milk
2 cups finely chopped hazelnuts, divided use
Sifted confectioners' sugar

Toast hazelnuts in a dry skillet over medium heat. When slightly brown and aromatic, remove from pan. Cool and then chop. Set aside.

Stir together flour, baking powder and salt in a medium mixing bowl. Set aside. Combine hazelnut spread and shortening in a large mixing bowl. Beat with an electric mixer until combined. Add sugar and beat until fluffy. Add vanilla, eggs and milk. Add flour mixture and beat until just combined. Stir in ½ cup of the hazelnuts. Cover and chill for several hours.

Preheat oven to 375 degrees.

Shape dough into 1-inch balls. Roll in a mixture of the remaining toasted hazelnuts and confectioners' sugar. Place balls 2 inches apart on ungreased cookie sheets. Bake 8 to 10 minutes.

KIM BAUMAN

Pecan Pick-Ups

PHOTO ON PAGE 124

MAKES:
36 bars.

FREEZEWORTHY:
So-so results because of the soft filling.

NOTES

These cookies make a tempting gift for the pecan lover. Cut into triangles for a more interesting presentation.

BASE:
½ cup (1 stick) unsalted butter, room temperature
¼ cup confectioners' sugar
1 cup all-purpose flour
Pinch of salt

FILLING:
1½ cups packed light brown sugar
2 eggs
2 tablespoons unsalted butter, melted
2 teaspoons vanilla
Pinch of salt
1 cup coarsely chopped pecans

Preheat oven to 350 degrees.

To make crust, blend butter, confectioners' sugar, flour and salt with fork. Pat into greased 9-inch square pan, covering only the bottom.
Bake 15 minutes. While baking, prepare filling.

To make the filling, combine brown sugar, eggs, butter, vanilla, salt and pecans, and then pour over partly baked crust. Bake 25 to 30 minutes, until set. Cool completely before cutting into bars.

KAREN HARAM, FOOD EDITOR,
SAN ANTONIO (TEXAS) EXPRESS-NEWS

Brandied Apricot Chews

PHOTO ON PAGE 120

MAKES:
About 2½ dozen.

FREEZEWORTHY:
The icing doesn't hold up in the freezer. Better to make these cookies and give away.

NOTES

The brandy extract in the icing is optional but it's what gives these distinctive cookies special flair.

1 cup (2 sticks) unsalted butter, room temperature
1 cup firmly packed brown sugar
1 egg
2½ cups quick-cooking rolled oats (not instant)
1 cup all-purpose flour
1 teaspoon baking soda
½ teaspoon salt
1 cup chopped dried apricots
½ cup chopped nuts

BRANDY ICING:
1¾ cups confectioners' sugar
2 tablespoons melted butter
2 tablespoons milk
2 teaspoons brandy extract
⅛ teaspoon salt

Preheat oven to 350 degrees.

Beat together butter and brown sugar until fluffy. Add egg. Combine dry ingredients and blend into butter-sugar-egg mixture. Stir in apricots and nuts.

Drop by rounded teaspoonful on ungreased cookie sheets. Bake for about 10 minutes, or until edges are light brown. Cool 1 minute on cookie sheets and then remove to wire rack. Cool completely.

To make the icing, combine ingredients until well blended and drizzle over cookies.

MARJORIE SCHNEIDER

Pistachio & Cherry Snowballs

PHOTO ON PAGE 125

MAKES:
5 dozen.

FREEZEWORTHY:
Yes, but cool completely first.

NOTES

A delicious and festive twist on traditional Mexican Wedding Cakes, these cookies are great for any occasion.

2 cups (4 sticks) unsalted butter, room temperature
1 cup confectioners' sugar, plus more for coating
2 tablespoons vanilla
1 teaspoon salt
1 cup shelled, unsalted natural pistachios, coarsely chopped
1 cup dried cherries (or cranberries)
3⅓ cups sifted cake flour
1⅔ cups sifted all-purpose flour

Preheat oven to 350 degrees. Grease large baking sheet, or line with parchment paper.

Beat butter and confectioners' sugar on medium-high until light and fluffy. Beat in vanilla and salt, and then add pistachios and cherries. Using spatula, mix in both flours; do not over mix.

Shape dough by generous tablespoons into football-shaped ovals. Place on baking sheets, spacing 1 inch apart. Bake cookies until bottoms just begin to brown, about 12 minutes. Cool on cookie sheet for 10 minutes.

Pour generous amount of confectioners' sugar into a bowl. Add a few warm cookies at a time and gently turn to coat thickly. Transfer to cooling rack or waxed paper. Repeat to coat cookies with sugar again. Cool completely.

KATHY HOCKER

TIP ***Most cookie recipes call for all-purpose flour but occasionally you'll see one like this that calls for cake flour. Cake flour has less gluten and protein and produces a more tender cookie.***

Heavenly Cream Wafers

PHOTO ON PAGE 120

MAKES:
2 to 3 dozen sandwich cookies.

FREEZEWORTHY:
No.

NOTES

This delicate, old-fashioned sandwich cookie will bring back memories for an older relative or teach a younger cook about baking way-back-when. Save this recipe for when you have some time.

WAFERS:

1 cup (2 sticks) unsalted butter, room temperature
⅓ cup heavy whipping cream
2 cups sifted all-purpose flour
Granulated sugar for rolling

BUTTER FILLING:

¼ cup unsalted butter, room temperature
¾ cup confectioners' sugar, sifted
1 teaspoon vanilla
Food coloring

Combine wafer ingredients. Chill at least one hour.

At least 10 minutes before baking, preheat oven to 375 degrees.

Roll out chilled dough to ⅛-inch thick. Cut into 1½-inch rounds. Transfer to waxed paper heavily sprinkled with granulated sugar, turning rounds with spatula to coat with sugar. Place on ungreased cookie sheet. Prick each round about four times with a fork. Bake until slightly puffy but not brown, 7 to 9 minutes. Let cool.

While wafers are cooling, make the filling by blending together softened butter, confectioners' sugar, 1 teaspoon vanilla and any color food coloring you like. If the filling seems too thick, add 1 teaspoon or less of milk. Once the wafers are cool, put two together with filling.

JANA BETH MIR

Raspberry Sugar Bars

PHOTO ON PAGE 122

MAKES:
12 to 15 bars.

FREEZEWORTHY:
No, they are too delicate to hold up to freezing and thawing.

NOTES

A flaky coconut top gives these bars a special look. Substitute other preserves if you like.

BASE:
¾ cup shortening
¼ cup sugar
¼ teaspoon salt
¼ teaspoon almond extract
1½ cups all-purpose flour
2 egg yolks

FILLING:
1 cup raspberry preserves
½ cup flaked coconut
2 egg whites, beaten
½ cup sugar

Preheat oven to 350 degrees.

For cookies, mix shortening, sugar, salt, almond extract, flour and egg yolks. Pat into 9-inch-by-13-inch ungreased pan and bake for 15 minutes.

For filling, spread preserves on crust while still hot, and top with coconut. Beat egg whites in a mixing bowl until peaks form and then add ½ cup sugar. Spread over coconut. Bake an additional 25 minutes. Cool on rack.

JADE HAMELRYCK

TIP ***While many modern cooks shy away from shortening because of its unhealthy reputation, most brands have been reformulated to eliminate trans-fats. Shortening makes cookies more tender.***

Oatmeal Carmelita Bars

PHOTO ON PAGE 123

MAKES:
2 dozen.

FREEZEWORTHY:
No.

NOTES

These are among my favorite recipes in this book. Rich and decadent, anyone would be happy to get a plate heaped with these treats.

BASE:
1½ cups all-purpose flour
1½ cups quick-cooking oats
¼ cup firmly packed brown sugar
½ teaspoon baking soda
¼ teaspoon salt
¾ cup (1½ sticks) unsalted butter, melted

FILLING:
1 cup chocolate chips
½ cup chopped pecans
3 tablespoons flour
¾ jar caramel ice cream topping or ¾ bag caramels melted with ¼ cup milk

Preheat oven to 350 degrees.

Combine all ingredients for the base in a large mixing bowl. Blend well until crumbs form. Press half of the crumbs onto the bottom of a 9-inch square pan. Bake for 10 minutes.

Remove from the oven.

Sprinkle with chocolate chips and pecans. Combine flour with caramel sauce and pour over chocolate chips and pecans. Sprinkle with remaining crumb mixture. Bake 15 to 20 minutes more or until golden brown.
Chill 1 to 2 hours. Cut into bars.

MARY-ANN JANSSEN AND GAYLE HACKBARTH

Cornmeal Cookies with Currants

PHOTO ON PAGE 123

MAKES: 4 to 5 dozen.

FREEZEWORTHY: Yes, but cool completely first.

NOTES

Give these to a foodie friend along with a selection of soothing teas. The cornmeal lends an interesting crunch to the cookies.

1½ cups all-purpose flour
1¼ cups yellow cornmeal
1 cup (2 sticks) unsalted butter, room temperature
1¼ cups sugar, divided use
¼ teaspoon salt
2 large egg yolks
1½ teaspoons vanilla
½ cup dried currants

Preheat oven to 350 degrees. Lightly grease cookie sheets.

Combine flour and cornmeal in a medium bowl. Beat butter, ¾ cup sugar and salt in a large mixing bowl at medium speed until light and fluffy. Add egg yolks and vanilla. Beat until well blended. Beat in the flour mixture at low speed just until combined. Beat in currants. Let dough stand 10 minutes.

Roll dough into 1-inch balls. Pour remaining ½ cup sugar into a shallow bowl. Roll each ball lightly in sugar. Arrange on cookie sheets, leaving about 2 inches between each sugared ball. Flatten to ¼-inch thickness with the bottom of a drinking glass dipped in the sugar.

Bake cookies until edges are golden brown, about 10 to 12 minutes. Cool cookies on baking sheets about 2 minutes. Transfer to racks and cool completely.

ROBIN DAVIS, FOOD EDITOR,
COLUMBUS (OHIO) DISPATCH

TIP *Invest in an offset spatula, which makes it easier to remove cookies from baking sheets.*

Strawberry Almond Bars

PHOTO ON PAGE 121

MAKES:
About 2 dozen.

FREEZEWORTHY:
Yes, but cool completely and cut first.

NOTES

This recipe can be easily doubled for a 9-inch-by-13-inch pan. Sprinkle more almonds on top. Then you are ready to split the batch with a new neighbor.

BASE:
½ cup (1 stick) unsalted butter
1 (10- to 12-ounce) package vanilla or white chips, divided
2 eggs
½ cup sugar
1 teaspoon almond extract
1 cup all-purpose flour
½ teaspoon salt

TOPPING:
½ cup seedless strawberry jam
¼ cup sliced almonds

Preheat oven to 325 degrees.

To make the base, melt butter in a 1-quart saucepan. Remove from heat and add 1 cup chips (do not stir). Beat eggs until foamy in a small mixing bowl; gradually add sugar. Stir in chip mixture and almond extract.

Combine flour and salt; add to egg mixture and stir just until combined. Spread half the batter in a greased 9-inch square baking pan.
Bake for 15 to 20 minutes or until golden brown.

To make topping, melt jam in a small saucepan over low heat; spread over warm crust. Stir remaining chips into the remaining batter; drop by teaspoonsful over the jam layer. Sprinkle with almonds. Bake 30 to 35 minutes longer or until a toothpick inserted near the center comes out clean. Cool on a wire rack.

RUTH M. DAUPER

Coconut Jam Bars

PHOTO ON PAGE 125

MAKES:
2 dozen.

FREEZEWORTHY:
No.

NOTES

This recipe gets a head start from a cake mix. Substitute strawberry or even mango preserves for a different twist.

BASE:
1 (18-ounce) package yellow cake mix
⅓ cup unsalted butter, cut in cubes
1 egg

TOPPING:
½ cup raspberry preserves
1 cup sugar
2 tablespoons butter, room temperature
3 eggs
2 tablespoons flour
¼ teaspoon baking powder
1½ cups flaked coconut

Heat oven to 350 degrees. Grease a 10-inch-by-15-inch jelly roll pan.

To make the base, combine cake mix, butter and egg in large bowl. Mix until crumbly. Press into prepared pan. Bake for 10 to 12 minutes. Cool slightly.

To make the topping, gently spread preserves over crust.

Mix sugar and softened butter in a medium bowl. Add eggs and beat well. Stir in flour and baking powder until blended. Fold in coconut. Pour over preserves and gently spread to cover.

Bake 15 to 20 minutes, or until light golden brown. Cool and cut into bars.

JOHN PACHECO

Orange Citrus Bars

PHOTO ON PAGE 123

MAKES:
About 2 dozen.

FREEZEWORTHY:
No.

NOTES

This gooey bar that makes good use of excess oranges or even tangerines is best eaten soon after making.

BASE:
2¼ cups all-purpose flour, divided use
½ cup confectioners' sugar
1 cup (2 sticks) unsalted butter, room temperature

FILLING:
2 cups granulated sugar
4 large eggs
Zest of 1 orange
⅓ cup orange juice
½ teaspoon baking powder
Confectioners' sugar (optional)

Preheat oven to 350 degrees.

To make base, combine 2 cups of the flour and confectioners' sugar in a large bowl. Cut in butter with a pastry blender until mixture is crumbly. Press evenly onto the bottom of a 13-inch-by-9-inch-by-2-inch baking pan. Bake 20 minutes, or until lightly browned.

To make the filling, whisk together granulated sugar, eggs, orange zest and juice in a medium bowl until well blended. Combine remaining ¼ cup flour and baking powder; add to sugar mixture, stirring to combine. Pour over hot baked crust and bake 25 more minutes, or until set. Sprinkle with confectioners' sugar, if desired.

SANDY MILLSPAUGH

Cherry Cheesecake Bars

PHOTO ON PAGE 121

MAKES:
About 25 bars.

FREEZEWORTHY:
No.

NOTES

Dried tropical fruits such as mango or pineapple can be used instead of the candied red and green cherries for a deliciously different bar.

BASE:
⅓ cup cold unsalted butter
⅓ cup brown sugar
1 cup all-purpose flour

FILLING:
1 (8-ounce) package cream cheese, softened
¼ cup sugar
1 egg
1 tablespoon lemon juice
½ cup chopped red and green candied cherries

Preheat oven to 350 degrees.

To make the base, cut butter into chunks and place in a 1-quart mixing bowl. Add brown sugar and flour; mix with an electric mixer at low speed, then medium speed, scraping sides of bowl until well mixed and crumbs form (about 1 minute). Remove ½ cup of mixture and set aside; press remaining crumb mixture into 8-inch square pan. Bake 10 to 12 minutes.

To make the filling, beat cream cheese, sugar, egg and lemon juice at medium speed until fluffy (1 to 2 minutes). Gently stir in cherries. Spread filling over slightly cooled crust and sprinkle with reserved crumb mixture. Continue baking 18 to 20 minutes or until filling is set and top is lightly browned. Cool. Store in the refrigerator.

ANN EZROW AND DONNA NELSON

TIP ❗ *Gather all ingredients before you start. The French call this mise en place (everything in its place), and it makes the cooking process much smoother because you aren't hunting for ingredients.*

Pineapple Scotch Bars

PHOTO ON PAGE 125

MAKES: 2 dozen.

FREEZEWORTHY: Yes, but cool completely first.

NOTES

Oats pressed into a fruity filling make these bars sturdy enough to pack for a long trip. Take them to your college student or grandmother a state away.

FILLING:

¼ cup sugar
1½ teaspoons cornstarch
1½ cups crushed pineapple, lightly drained
3 tablespoons apricot jam

BASE:

1½ cups sifted all-purpose flour
½ teaspoon baking soda
½ teaspoon salt
1½ cups quick-cooking rolled oats (not instant)
1 cup brown sugar, packed
¾ cup shortening

Preheat oven to 375 degrees.

To make filling, blend sugar and cornstarch in a 2-quart saucepan. Add pineapple with jam, stirring well to combine. Cook and stir over low heat until clear and thick. Cool while making crust.

To make base, sift together flour, baking soda and salt. Mix with oats and brown sugar. Work in shortening until mixture is crumbly. Pat half into a 9-inch square pan. Spread with filling. Press rest of crumbly mix onto filling, pressing it in so the oats will not flake off and become dry.

Bake for 35 to 40 minutes. Cool and cut into bars.

JOHN PACHECO

CHAPTER 3

CHOCOLATE!

FOR CHOCOHOLICS AND THE PEOPLE WHO LOVE THEM AND BAKE FOR THEM

It is a rare soul who doesn't like chocolate, and even those who say they aren't fans just might gobble up a chocolate chip cookie straight from the oven.

For the recipes in this chapter, use the chocolate designated. Semisweet is not the same as unsweetened, nor is German chocolate the same as white chocolate, which purists say isn't really chocolate at all.

These recipes pair chocolate with some of their most amiable partners. That list includes peanut butter, marshmallow, citrus and, of course, nuts. We love to include them but make no mistake, chocolate is the dominant flavor. The more, the better, I say.

CHOCOLATE! COOKIES

Coconut Chocolate Clusters

PHOTO ON PAGE 131

MAKES:
3 dozen.

FREEZEWORTHY:
No. But, these will keep in the refrigerator for up to one week.

NOTES

These no-bake cookies are held together with oatmeal, peanut butter and coconut. Give them even more texture with chunky peanut butter.

2 cups sugar
½ cup unsweetened cocoa powder
½ cup milk
½ cup (1 stick) unsalted butter
2 cups old-fashioned oatmeal
½ cup peanut butter
½ cup flaked coconut
1 teaspoon vanilla

Mix sugar, cocoa powder, milk and butter in a 2-quart saucepan; bring to a boil. Remove from heat, add remaining ingredients. Stir well to combine. Drop by teaspoonful onto waxed paper. Chill.

HELEN WEST

TIP **!** ***Don't be tempted to swap chocolates in a recipe. If you substitute milk chocolate for semisweet the result may be cookies that taste too sweet and lack chocolate flavor.***

White Chocolate Cranberry Drops

PHOTO ON PAGE 129

MAKES:
4 dozen.

FREEZEWORTHY:
Yes, but cool completely first.

NOTES

These are so sweet that they are just as good without the glaze. Consider baking them for the long Thanksgiving weekend when your guests need something to nibble the day after turkey.

1⅔ cups flour
1 teaspoon ground cinnamon
1 teaspoon baking powder
¼ teaspoon baking soda
¼ teaspoon salt
1 cup (2 sticks) unsalted butter, room temperature
1 cup packed light brown sugar
1½ teaspoons finely grated orange zest
1 large egg
2½ teaspoons vanilla
1½ cups coarsely chopped pecans
1½ cups chopped dried sweetened cranberries
1½ cups white chocolate morsels
½ cup chopped cranberries

ICING:
1 cup sifted confectioners' sugar
1 tablespoon lemon juice
⅛ teaspoon vanilla
2 to 4 teaspoons warm water

Preheat oven to 350 degrees. Lightly grease baking pans or line with parchment paper.

Combine flour, cinnamon, baking powder, baking soda and salt in a large mixing bowl; set aside.

Beat butter in a medium mixing bowl for several minutes until light. Add brown sugar and orange zest beating to incorporate and then add egg and vanilla. Beat for 2 minutes. With mixer on low speed, add flour mixture in increments until smoothly incorporated. Stir in pecans, dried cranberries, white chocolate morsels and chopped cranberries, taking care that they are evenly distributed.

Drop dough by heaping tablespoonsful, spaced about 2½ inches apart on baking sheets. Bake cookies, one sheet at a time, for 8 to 10 minutes. Cool cookies on sheets for about 3 minutes, then carefully transfer to a wire rack. Cookies will be very tender. Cool completely.

To make the icing, combine confectioners' sugar, lemon juice and vanilla in a medium bowl. Add enough water to make the icing slightly runny. Transfer to a pastry bag fitted with fine tip, or use a spoon to immediately drizzle the icing in very fine lines over the cookies until they are lightly decorated. Let them stand until icing sets, at least one hour.

ELAINE PATENAUDE

Buckeyes in the Pan

PHOTO ON PAGE 127

MAKES: About 35 squares.

FREEZEWORTHY: Yes, but cool completely first.

NOTES

This is a timesaver for making Ohio's favorite chocolate-peanut butter cookie-candy, the buckeye.

BASE:
1 cup (2 sticks) unsalted butter, room temperature
1 cup peanut butter
2 cups graham cracker crumbs
2½ cups confectioners' sugar

TOP LAYER:
10 ounces chocolate chips
6 tablespoons vegetable oil

To make the base, mix butter with peanut butter in a large mixing bowl. Add graham cracker crumbs and confectioners' sugar; combine well. Pat into 9-inch-by-13-inch pan. Set aside.

To make the top layer, melt chocolate chips over low heat and then stir in vegetable oil until well combined. Pour over top of graham cracker crust and refrigerate until set.

SHIRLEY ZAGORC

TIP *Make life easier by purchasing graham cracker crumbs in a box. They are easy to measure and handy to have on hand.*

Black Mountain Cookies

PHOTO ON PAGE 126

MAKES: 3 dozen.

FREEZEWORTHY: No.

NOTES

Ooey, gooey and lots of fun, this cookie is truly a mountain of chocolate. It is a close cousin of the fireside s'more, but the beauty — you can make them indoors.

12 large marshmallows
1¾ cups all-purpose flour
½ teaspoon baking soda
1 cup sugar
½ cup baking cocoa
½ teaspoon salt
½ cup soft shortening
2 tablespoons water
½ cup evaporated milk
1 egg
1 teaspoon vanilla
½ cup chopped walnuts

FROSTING:
1 cup semisweet chocolate chips
½ cup evaporated milk
2½ cups confectioners' sugar

Preheat oven to 350 degrees.

Cut marshmallows horizontally into thirds. Set aside.

Sift flour, baking soda, sugar, cocoa and salt into a large bowl.
Add shortening, water, evaporated milk, egg and vanilla; beat with an electric mixer for 3 minutes at low speed. Stir in walnuts.
Drop by tablespoonsful onto greased cookie sheet. Bake 10 minutes.
Immediately after removing from oven, place one marshmallow slice on each cookie, cut side down. Cool cookies on rack.

While cookies cool, make frosting by stirring chocolate chips and evaporated milk in a 2-quart saucepan over low heat. Add confectioners' sugar after the chocolate is melted. Stir until smooth. Spoon frosting over cookies to cover the marshmallows.

MARLENE HAGSTROM

Chocolate Walnut Puffs

PHOTO ON PAGE 127

MAKES: About 3 dozen.

FREEZEWORTHY: Yes, but cool completely first.

NOTES

For delicious variations, substitute almond or peppermint extracts for vanilla. These are quite delicate and, yes, there is no flour!

1 (6-ounce) package semisweet chocolate chips
2 egg whites
⅛ teaspoon salt
½ cup granulated sugar
½ teaspoon vanilla
½ teaspoon vinegar
¾ cup chopped walnuts

Preheat oven to 350 degrees.

Melt chocolate chips in a double boiler over hot (not boiling) water.

In a mixing bowl, beat egg whites with salt until foamy. Gradually add sugar and beat until stiff peaks form. Beat in vanilla and vinegar. Fold in melted chocolate and walnuts.

Drop by teaspoonful onto greased cookie sheet. Bake for 10 minutes. Remove from cookie sheets immediately.

FLORENCE TIRABASSI

TIP *Just a drop of moisture can cause melted chocolate to become lumpy. If this should happen, stir in 1 tablespoon of vegetable shortening for every 3 ounces of chocolate. Do not use butter, as it contains water.*

Mint Chocolate Cookies

PHOTO ON PAGE 128

MAKES:
3 to 4 dozen.

FREEZEWORTHY:
Yes, but cool completely first.

NOTES

Refreshing and satisfying, these cookies could provide the sandwich bookends for a scoop of mint-chocolate chip ice cream.

1 cup (2 sticks) unsalted butter, room temperature
1¾ cups sugar
2 large eggs
¾ teaspoon peppermint extract
2 cups all-purpose flour
1 cup unsweetened cocoa powder
1 teaspoon baking soda
½ teaspoon baking powder
½ teaspoon salt
Confectioners' sugar for sprinkling

Using electric mixer, beat butter and sugar in a large bowl until well blended. Beat in eggs and peppermint extract. Set aside.

Mix flour, cocoa powder, baking soda, baking powder and salt in a separate large bowl until blended (use a wire sieve if you'd like). Add these dry ingredients to butter and sugar mixture beating well until blended. Chill dough about an hour.

About 10 minutes before baking, preheat oven to 350 degrees.

Remove dough from refrigerator and form into 1-inch balls (use a melon baller for uniform cookies). Place 2 inches apart on prepared baking sheets. Flatten balls slightly to 1½-inch rounds. Bake cookies for 5 minutes until edges begin to firm but center still appears soft. Remove from oven and transfer to wire racks to cool completely.

Cookies can be prepared up to five days ahead and stored in an airtight container at room temperature or frozen for several weeks. Cookies can also be stored in an airtight container in the refrigerator; add a slice of white bread to keep cookies moist.

Before serving, sift confectioners' sugar over the cookies.

DIANE C. SHARP

Chocolate Yum-Yums

PHOTO ON PAGE 126

MAKES: 4 dozen.

FREEZEWORTHY: Yes, but cool completely first.

NOTES

Tiny cupcake-like cookies look festive when served in paper liners.

1 (6-ounce) package semisweet chocolate chips
1 cup (2 sticks) unsalted butter (or ½ cup butter and ½ cup margarine)
2 cups chopped nuts
1¾ cups sugar
4 eggs, slightly beaten
1 cup all-purpose flour
2 teaspoons vanilla
Confectioners' sugar (optional)

Preheat oven to 325 degrees.

Melt chocolate chips with butter in a 1-quart saucepan over low heat; mix in nuts. Transfer to a large mixing bowl and add sugar, eggs, flour and vanilla; mix well. Line small muffin tins with paper or foil cups, then fill two-thirds with batter.

Bake for 25 minutes. Do not over bake; insides should still be soft. Sprinkle with confectioners' sugar before serving, if desired.

PAT GESNAKER

TIP *Preheat oven for 10 to 15 minutes before you start baking unless the recipe directs you to do otherwise.*

Triple Chocolate Hazelnut Biscotti

PHOTO ON PAGE 128

MAKES:
3 to 4 dozen.

FREEZEWORTHY:
Yes, but cool completely first.

NOTES

Coat hands lightly with oil or spritz with nonstick spray before handling dough to keep it from sticking. To drizzle melted white chocolate, place it in a sealable plastic bag and snip a corner. This controls the drizzle better.

8 ounces chopped white chocolate
6 tablespoons unsalted butter, room temperature
1 cup brown sugar
2 eggs
1 teaspoon vanilla
2 cups all-purpose flour
½ cup cocoa powder
1 teaspoon baking soda
1 teaspoon salt
1 cup skinned, toasted hazelnuts, roughly chopped
1 cup semisweet chocolate mini chips

Preheat oven to 350 degrees. Line one baking sheet with parchment and set aside. Set a steel bowl over a saucepan of simmering water. Add the chopped white chocolate to the bowl and turn off the heat. Stir occasionally. Set aside for drizzling over baked cookies.

In large bowl of a stand mixer, cream butter with brown sugar until fluffy. Beat in eggs, one at a time. Beat in vanilla.

In another bowl, combine with a whisk the flour, cocoa, baking soda and salt. With the mixer at low speed, add the dry ingredients to the butter mixture. Mix until just incorporated, then stop the mixer. Pour in the hazelnuts and chocolate chips. Turn the mixer back on to medium, and let the paddle go only about six or seven revolutions.

Divide the dough in half. Create two long, flattened logs, slightly squared on the sides (about 12 inches long) on the sheet pan. (Squaring the sides prevents the edges of the biscotti from breaking off during slicing.) Bake the logs about 40 minutes on the baking sheet. Cool long enough to handle, about 12 minutes.

Slice the biscotti with a serrated knife on a cutting board into ¾-inch slices and arrange, cut-side down, on the baking sheet. Return the biscotti to the oven for about 10 minutes. Turn them to crisp the other side and bake another 5 minutes. Let the biscotti cool completely.

Drizzle biscotti with the melted white chocolate. Let the chocolate set before serving.

LOUISE "CHIFFONADE" BRESCIA

Chocolate Snowballs

PHOTO ON PAGE 130

MAKES:
About 7 dozen.

FREEZEWORTHY:
Yes, but cool completely first. Roll in confectioners' sugar again before serving.

NOTES

These puffs of chocolate get deep flavor from unsweetened cocoa. Use the highest quality you can afford for best results.

1¼ cups (2½ sticks) unsalted butter, room temperature
⅔ cup granulated sugar
2 teaspoons vanilla
2 cups all-purpose flour
½ cup unsweetened cocoa
¼ teaspoon salt
½ cup finely chopped pecans
Sifted confectioners' sugar

Preheat oven to 350 degrees.

Beat butter in a bowl with an electric mixer at medium speed until creamy. Gradually add sugar and vanilla. Combine flour, cocoa, salt and nuts in a separate bowl. Gradually add to butter mixture and beat until blended.

Portion dough by teaspoonsful and roll into balls. Place on ungreased baking sheets. Bake for 8 to 10 minutes. Roll warm cookies in confectioners' sugar.

JERI EMERY

TIP *If cookies frequently burn in your oven, it may be that the oven thermostat is off. An oven thermometer can verify the temperature.*

Crème de Menthe Chocolate Squares

PHOTO ON PAGE 131

MAKES:
20 to 25 squares.

FREEZEWORTHY:
No. The added moisture from thawing will turn the bars to goo.

NOTES

Perfectly decadent and plenty gooey, this is the recipe to make when you want to be very, very bad.

BROWNIE LAYER:
1 cup granulated sugar
½ cup (1 stick) unsalted butter, room temperature
4 eggs, beaten
1 cup all-purpose flour
½ teaspoon salt
1 teaspoon vanilla
1 (16-ounce) can chocolate syrup

CREME DE MENTHE LAYER:
2 cups confectioners' sugar, sifted
3 tablespoons crème de menthe liqueur
½ cup unsalted butter, melted

CHOCOLATE GLAZE:
6 ounces semisweet mini chocolate chips
6 tablespoons unsalted butter

Preheat oven to 350 degrees.

In a large bowl, cream together sugar and butter. Add beaten eggs and blend well. Add flour and salt; mix well. Blend in vanilla and chocolate syrup. Pour batter into a greased 9-inch-by-13-inch-by-2-inch baking pan. Bake for 25 to 30 minutes. Cool in pan.

For crème de menthe layer, mix confectioners' sugar, crème de menthe and butter, then pour over cooled brownies.

For chocolate glaze layer, melt chocolate chips and butter together in a 1-quart saucepan over low heat, stirring until smooth. Cool mixture for 3 minutes, and then spread over mint layer. Chill until ready to serve, and then cut into small squares.

SUE E. CONRAD AND MARGIE SAMBETS

Crunchy Fudge Bars

PHOTO ON PAGE 131

MAKES:
2 dozen.

FREEZEWORTHY:
No. The Rice Krispies® will lose their snap, crackle and pop.

NOTES

Here is another no-bake recipe that will satisfy your sweet tooth without disrupting your busy schedule.

1 cup butterscotch chips
½ cup peanut butter
4 cups Rice Krispies® cereal
1 tablespoon water
1 cup semisweet chocolate chips
½ cup sifted confectioners' sugar
2 tablespoons margarine or butter

Melt butterscotch chips with peanut butter in a heavy saucepan over low heat, stirring constantly until well blended. Remove from heat and add Rice Krispies® cereal. Stir until cereal is well coated. Press half of cereal mixture into buttered 8-inch square pan. Chill in refrigerator. Set aside remaining cereal mixture.

Combine water, chocolate chips, sugar and margarine or butter in a double boiler or small saucepan set over hot water, stirring until chocolate melts. Spread over chilled cereal crust, and then spread remaining cereal mixture evenly on top and press in gently. Chill.

Remove from refrigerator about 10 minutes before cutting into squares.

SANDY GATEWOOD

TIP *For sticky bar cookies, use the back of a large spoon or measuring cup that has been buttered or spritzed with non-stick spray to press the mixture into the pan.*

Chocolate-Mint Crème Cookies

PHOTO ON PAGE 129

MAKES:
4 dozen.

FREEZEWORTHY:
No.

NOTES

This classic combination is a show-stopping sandwich cookie that combines cooling mint with chocolate.

1½ cups packed brown sugar
¾ cup unsalted butter, cubed
2 tablespoons water
2 cups semisweet chocolate chips
2 eggs
3 cups all-purpose flour
1¼ teaspoons baking soda
1 teaspoon salt

FILLING:
⅓ cup unsalted butter, room temperature
3 cups confectioners' sugar
3 tablespoons milk
⅛ teaspoon peppermint extract
Dash salt

Preheat oven to 350 degrees.

In a small saucepan, combine the brown sugar, butter and water. Cook and stir over medium heat until sugar is dissolved. Remove from the heat; stir in the chocolate chips until melted and smooth. Transfer to a large mixing bowl; cool slightly.

Add eggs, one at a time, beating well after each addition. Combine the flour, baking soda and salt in a medium mixing bowl; gradually add to chocolate mixture. Drop by rounded teaspoonful onto greased baking sheets. Bake for 8 to 10 minutes or until set. Remove to wire racks; flatten slightly. Cool completely.

Combine filling ingredients in a large mixing bowl, beating until smooth; spread on the bottom of half of the cookies. Top with remaining cookie halves. Store in the refrigerator.

This Little Piggy Had a Cookie

PHOTO ON PAGE 129

MAKES: 3 dozen.

FREEZEWORTHY: Yes, but cool completely first.

NOTES

Maple-cured bacon lends a back note to this cookie that's irresistible.

6 slices maple-cured bacon, chopped
1½ cups sugar
1 cup (2 sticks) butter, room temperature
2 eggs
2 teaspoons vanilla
2 cups all-purpose flour
⅔ cup cocoa powder
½ teaspoon baking soda
¼ teaspoon salt
2 cups semisweet chocolate chunks

Preheat an oven to 350 degrees.

Place bacon in a large, deep skillet, and fry over medium-high heat, turning occasionally, until evenly browned, about 10 minutes. Drain on a paper towel-lined plate. Crumble. Set aside.

Beat the sugar, butter, eggs, and vanilla with an electric mixer in a large bowl until fluffy and smooth. Stir in flour, cocoa powder, baking soda, and salt. Stir in the chocolate chips and bacon. Drop cookies by rounded spoonfuls onto ungreased cookie sheets.

Bake for 10 to 12 minutes. Let stand 5 minutes before transferring to wire racks to cool completely.

TIP ***Use heavy-gauge aluminum cookie sheets with a reflective surface. They should be rimless. Dark sheets will make your cookies darker on the bottom and they will burn more easily. Rimmed baking sheets deflect heat and facilitate uneven cooking.***

Chocolate Crunch Morsels

PHOTO ON PAGE 128

MAKES:
At least 8 dozen but you may need to discard the outer edges if they become too hard.

FREEZEWORTHY:
Yes, but cool completely.

NOTES

A home-made caramel sauce is an extra step and macadamia nuts a splurge but worth the investment. Cut these morsels into very small squares — they're that rich. Use a food processor to chop the nuts but don't grind too fine. Because the mixture tends to bubble over while baking, line the lower rack in your oven with foil to catch drips.

BASE:
3 cups graham cracker crumbs
¾ cup (1½ stick) unsalted butter, melted
½ cup sugar
1 (24-ounce) bag chocolate chips
2 cups flaked coconut

CARAMEL TOPPING:
2 cups (4 sticks) butter, room temperature
1 cup light corn syrup
3 cups packed brown sugar
¼ cup heavy cream
1 teaspoon vanilla
5 cups (about 24 ounces) coarsely chopped macadamia nuts

Preheat oven to 325 degrees.

Combine graham cracker crumbs, sugar and butter; press into an 11-inch-by-17-inch metal baking pan. (It's sometimes called a full sheet pan.) Sprinkle evenly with chocolate chips and coconut.

Combine remaining butter, syrup and brown sugar in a heavy, 5-quart saucepan. Cook over low heat until butter melts, stirring with a wooden spoon. Increase heat and bring to a boil. Boil for 3 minutes. Remove pan from heat and stir in cream and vanilla. (Be careful because caramel may boil up.). Stir in nuts. Pour into sheet pan carefully making sure to distribute the nuts and sauce evenly.

Bake 25 minutes or until center is set. Lower temperature if outer edges brown too quickly. Cool completely and then chill overnight. Cut into small bars.

LENNIE BENNETT

Hot Chocolate Balls

PHOTO ON PAGE 131

MAKES:
About 4 dozen.

FREEZEWORTHY:
Yes, but cool completely first.

NOTES

These cookies taste just like a cup of hot chocolate. Try them with a shake or two of cayenne pepper in the dough.

1 cup (2 sticks) unsalted butter, room temperature
1¼ cups confectioners' sugar, divided use
½ cup unsweetened cocoa powder, divided use
1 teaspoon vanilla
2 cups all-purpose flour
1½ teaspoons ground cinnamon, divided use
½ cup toasted pecans, finely chopped

Preheat oven to 325 degrees.

Beat butter in a large mixing bowl with an electric mixer on medium to high speed for 30 seconds. Beat in ½ cup confectioners' sugar, ¼ cup cocoa powder and vanilla until combined, scraping side of bowl occasionally. Beat in as much flour as you can with the mixer; stir in the remaining flour, 1 teaspoon cinnamon and pecans.

Shape dough into 1-inch balls and then place 2 inches apart on ungreased cookie sheets. Bake for 18 to 20 minutes or until bottoms are lightly browned. Transfer cookies to wire racks and cool completely.

Combine remaining confectioners' sugar, cocoa powder and cinnamon in a small bowl. Roll cooled cookies in the sugar mixture.

LINDA SPURGUS

Fudgy Citrus Cookies

PHOTO ON PAGE 127

MAKES: About 4 dozen.

FREEZEWORTHY: Yes, but cool completely first.

NOTES

Chocolate is an amiable companion with citrus and this cookie gets a boost from the fresh juice and zest of orange and lime.

2 ¼ cups all-purpose flour
½ cup unsweetened Dutch-process cocoa powder
1 teaspoon baking soda
¼ teaspoon salt
Zest and juice of 1 orange, divided use
Zest and juice of 1 lime, divided use
1 cup (2 sticks) unsalted butter, room temperature
¾ cup plus 1 tablespoon granulated sugar, divided use
1 cup tightly packed dark brown sugar
2 large eggs
1 cup chocolate chips

Preheat oven to 350 degrees.

Sift flour, cocoa, baking soda and salt together into a bowl and set aside. In a small bowl mix orange and lime zest with 1 tablespoon sugar. Set aside.

In a large mixing bowl or the bowl of an electric mixer fitted with paddle attachment, cream together the butter and both sugars until light in color and fluffy, about 2 minutes. Add the eggs, one at a time, beating well after each addition and scraping down the sides of the bowl. Beat in the orange and lime juice.

Stir in the flour mixture in three additions, blending just until the dry ingredients are moistened. Stir in the zest mixture and chocolate chips; mix gently until evenly distributed.

Drop the batter by heaping tablespoonsful onto parchment-paper lined baking sheets and place them in the center of the oven. Bake for 15 to 18 minutes, or until barely set in the center and just firm around the edges. Cool on sheets for about 5 minutes then transfer to wire racks.

Caramel Bars

PHOTO ON PAGE 130

MAKES:
14 to 20 bars.

FREEZEWORTHY:
So-so results. The caramel is likely to be runny after thawing.

NOTES

An oatmeal-laced base helps to hold the sticky-sweet store-bought caramel topping. How many bars you'll get from a batch depends on how big you cut them.

BASE:
1 cup old-fashioned oatmeal (not instant)
1 cup all-purpose flour
½ teaspoon baking soda
¾ cup (1½ sticks) unsalted butter, room temperature
¾ cup brown sugar

FILLING:
1 cup chocolate chips
1 (12-ounce) jar caramel topping
3 tablespoons all-purpose flour
½ cup chopped nuts

Preheat oven to 350 degrees.

To make the base, mix all base ingredients together in a large bowl. Save half of the mixture for the top of bars. Press the other half into an 8-inch square pan that has been lightly coated with a nonstick baking spray. Bake for 10 to 15 minutes.

Meanwhile, make the filling by combining all the filling ingredients. Spread over baked base and top with remaining unbaked mixture. Return pan to oven and bake an additional 30 minutes. Cool and then firm in the fridge.

CAROLYN SMILEY

TIP ***Bake bars and squares in greased pans that are at least 1½ inches deep.***

Chocolate Macaroon Meringue Bites

PHOTO ON PAGE 131

MAKES:
40 to 60 bars.

FREEZEWORTHY:
Not recommended.

NOTES

A delicate baked meringue topping gives these bars an elegant touch. Make sure to whip the eggs whites and brown sugar until they are very stiff before covering the macaroon batter.

FIRST LAYER:

¾ cup (1½ sticks) unsalted butter, room temperature
½ cup packed brown sugar
½ cup sugar
3 yolks
1 teaspoon vanilla
2 cups all-purpose flour
1 teaspoon baking powder
¼ teaspoon baking soda
¼ teaspoon salt

SECOND LAYER:

1 (6-ounce) package semisweet chocolate pieces
1 cup shredded coconut
¾ cup coarsely chopped nuts

THIRD LAYER:

3 egg whites
1 cup packed brown sugar

Preheat oven to 350 degrees. Grease a 9-inch-by-13-inch baking pan; set aside.

Cream butter, sugars, egg yolks and vanilla. Beat 2 minutes on medium speed, scraping bowl constantly. Blend flour, baking powder, baking soda and salt together in a separate bowl, then add to butter mixture. Spread or pat dough into pan. Sprinkle with chocolate chips, coconut and nuts. Set aside.

Beat egg whites until frothy; gradually add 1 cup brown sugar; beat until stiff. Spread over nut mixture. Bake for 35 to 40 minutes. Cool and then cut into bars.

Choco-Coco Pecan Crisps

PHOTO ON PAGE 126

MAKES: About 3 dozen.

FREEZEWORTHY: Yes, but cool completely first.

NOTES

This dough is super-stiff. A sturdy spoon might not be enough to mix it thoroughly. Wash your hands, and well, plunge right in!

½ cup (1 stick) unsalted butter, room temperature
1 cup packed light brown sugar
1 egg
1 teaspoon vanilla
1½ cups all-purpose flour
1 cup chopped pecans
⅓ cup unsweetened cocoa
½ teaspoon baking soda
1 cup flaked coconut

Cream butter and sugar in a large mixing bowl until fluffy. Beat in egg and vanilla. Set aside.

Combine flour, pecans, cocoa and baking soda in small bowl; mix well. Add to creamed butter mixture, blending until stiff dough is formed.

Sprinkle coconut on work surface. Divide dough into four parts. Shape each into a roll about 1½-inches in diameter; roll in coconut until thickly coated. Wrap rolls in plastic wrap and refrigerate until firm, at least one hour or up to two weeks. You can wrap in foil and freeze up to six weeks.

About 10 minutes before baking, preheat oven to 350 degrees. Slice cookie rolls ¼-inch thick and bake on an ungreased cookie sheets for 10 to 12 minutes.

LAURA PETERSON

Chewy Chocolate Orange Nuggets

PHOTO ON PAGE 128

MAKES:
3 to 4 dozen.

FREEZEWORTHY:
Yes, but cool completely first.

NOTES

Demerara sugar is a large crystal, raw sugar that is generally brown. It lends a specific flavor to the cookie but you can substitute another type of sugar.

10 ounces dark sweet chocolate, chopped
6 ounces unsweetened chocolate, chopped
¾ cup (1½ sticks) unsalted butter
2 cups sugar
6 large eggs
2 teaspoons vanilla
1 teaspoon orange extract
2 tablespoons orange zest
2 cups sifted all-purpose flour
1 teaspoon salt
10 ounces milk chocolate, chopped
Chocolate sprinkles or demerara sugar

Preheat oven to 375 degrees.

In a double boiler, melt the dark sweet chocolate, the unsweetened chocolate and the butter. Stir until all lumps are gone. Set aside for 10 minutes to cool. Combine chocolate mix with sugar and beat on medium-high speed for 5 minutes, scraping sides often. Add eggs and combine thoroughly. Add vanilla, orange extract and zest, mixing well to incorporate. Add flour and salt, and mix well on low speed. Stir in the chopped milk chocolate by hand.

Line cookie sheets with parchment paper or Silpat® sheets. Using a 2-inch scoop, form dough into balls and place about 1½ inches apart on cookie sheets. Press sprinkles or demerara sugar onto the cookies. Bake 9 to 11 minutes, rotating sheets halfway through.

LISA BAZZANELLA SMITH

Mocha Truffle Cookies

PHOTO ON PAGE 131

MAKES: 3½ dozen.

FREEZEWORTHY: Yes, but cool completely first.

NOTES

Instant coffee intensifies chocolate flavor in these cookies. The melted chips combined with whole ones don't hurt either.

½ cup unsalted butter or margarine
1½ cups semisweet chocolate chips, divided use
1 tablespoon instant coffee granules
¾ cup sugar
¾ cup packed brown sugar
2 eggs
2 teaspoons vanilla
2 cups all-purpose flour
⅓ cup unsweetened cocoa powder
½ teaspoon baking powder
¼ teaspoon salt

Preheat oven to 350 degrees.

Melt butter or margarine and ½ cup chocolate chips in a large saucepan over low heat. Stir until smooth and well combined. Remove from heat. Stir in coffee granules; cool 5 minutes. Stir in sugar, brown sugar, eggs and vanilla. Set aside.

Combine flour, cocoa powder, baking powder and salt in a medium mixing bowl. Stir into chocolate-coffee mixture. Stir in the remaining cup of chocolate chips. Drop dough by rounded tablespoonsful onto lightly greased cookie sheets. Bake for 10 minutes. Let cool 1 minute on cookie sheet. Remove and cool completely on wire racks.

GAYLE HACKBARTH

TIP ***Read recipes twice before preparing a shopping list. And, unless you are an experienced baker, don't experiment until you've made the basic recipe at least once.***

Chocolate Coffee Batons

PHOTO ON PAGE 126

MAKES: About 3 dozen.

FREEZEWORTHY: Yes, but cool completely first.

NOTES

These finger-shaped cookies have a pleasant crunch, plus a nutty chocolate dip at the end gives them a toffee-like taste. This dough is quite crumbly. Don't panic; just force it together as you roll.

2¼ cups all-purpose flour
¼ cup light brown sugar, firmly packed
½ cup granulated sugar
½ cup (1 stick) lightly salted or unsalted butter, room temperature
¼ cup heavy cream
1 tablespoon instant-coffee granules
½ teaspoon salt
½ teaspoon baking powder

FOR DIPPING:
1 cup semisweet chocolate chips
2 teaspoons solid vegetable shortening
1½ cups finely chopped almonds, pecans, walnuts or hazelnuts

Put flour, sugars, butter, cream, coffee granules, salt and baking powder in the large bowl of an electric mixer and beat until thoroughly blended. Cover dough and chill 1 hour or longer, until firm enough to shape.

Preheat oven to 375 degrees.

Using a rounded teaspoonful for each, roll dough into 3-inch-by-½-inch logs; place 2 inches apart on an ungreased cookie sheet. Bake about 7 minutes, until golden brown. Cool on a wire rack.

To make the dipping chocolate, melt chocolate chips with shortening in a double boiler or in the microwave. Stir well to combine. Dip ends of cooled cookies in melted chocolate and then in chopped nuts.

RUTH LANGAN

Death by Chocolate Cookies

PHOTO ON PAGE 129

MAKES:
12 large cookies or about 24 smaller ones.

FREEZEWORTHY:
Yes, but cool completely first.

NOTES

One taste and you will understand why this simple cookie has its name. It delivers a wicked chocolate kick, thanks to deep-brown dough studded with heavenly chunks of chocolate.

16 ounces semisweet chocolate
¾ cup firmly packed dark brown sugar
¼ cup (½ stick) unsalted butter, melted
2 eggs
1 teaspoon vanilla
½ cup flour
¼ teaspoon baking powder

Preheat oven to 350 degrees.

Coarsely chop the chocolate. Set aside half. Place the remaining chocolate in a medium-sized microwave-safe bowl. Microwave on high 1 to 2 minutes or until melted. Stir until chocolate is melted and smooth.

Combine brown sugar, butter, eggs and vanilla in a mixing bowl, and then stir into melted chocolate. Stir in flour and baking powder. When well combined, stir in reserved chopped chocolate. (The batter will resemble brownie batter.) Drop by the ¼ cup or rounded tablespoon for smaller cookies onto ungreased cookie sheets. Bake until puffed and center feels set to touch, about 11 minutes for large cookies, 7 to 9 for smaller cookies.

ROBIN DAVIS, FOOD EDITOR,
COLUMBUS (OHIO) DISPATCH

Tropical White Chocolate Cookies

PHOTO ON PAGE 131

MAKES:
About 4 dozen.

FREEZEWORTHY:
Yes, but cool completely first.

NOTES

Citrus and white chocolate, along with the salty kick of macadamia nuts and chewy flakes of coconut, give these cookies ramped-up flavor.

¾ cup (1½ sticks) unsalted butter, room temperature
¾ cup firmly packed brown sugar
¾ cup granulated sugar
1 teaspoon vanilla
2 large eggs
3 teaspoons grated lime zest
2 tablespoons fresh lime juice
2½ cups all-purpose flour
1 teaspoon baking soda
½ teaspoon salt
1 (12-ounce) package white chocolate chips
1½ cups sweetened flaked coconut
½ cup chopped macadamia nuts

Preheat oven to 375 degrees.

Beat first four ingredients in a large mixing bowl at medium speed with an electric mixer until creamy. Add eggs, beating until blended. Add lime zest and juice. Set aside.

Combine flour, baking soda and salt in a small bowl; gradually add to butter-egg mixture, beating well. Stir in white chocolate chips, coconut and macadamia nuts. Drop by rounded tablespoonsful onto ungreased baking sheets and bake for 10 to 12 minutes or until lightly brown.
Cool on wire racks.

MARY-ANN JANSSEN

Chocolate Cins

PHOTO ON PAGE 127

MAKES:
2 dozen.

FREEZEWORTHY:
Yes, but cool completely first.

NOTES

A bit of the cinnamon in the dough elevates chocolate cookies to something special. Substitute another type of nut for the walnuts, if you'd like. I am always partial to pecans, especially when they are toasted.

4 (1-ounce) semisweet chocolate squares
½ cup packed brown sugar
3 tablespoons vegetable oil
1 egg
½ teaspoon vanilla
½ cup all-purpose flour
½ teaspoon baking powder
¼ teaspoon salt
¼ teaspoon cinnamon
½ cup chopped walnuts
½ cup confectioners' sugar

Melt chocolate squares on low in a 1-quart saucepan. Remove from heat.

Blend brown sugar and oil with a fork in large mixing bowl. Add egg and beat well with fork. Stir in vanilla. Add flour, baking powder, salt and cinnamon. Stir in melted chocolate and nuts. Chill dough for at least 1 hour.

Preheat oven to 350 degrees.

Drop dough by rounded teaspoonful into confectioners' sugar. Roll to coat dough. Place 2 inches apart on nonstick cookie sheet. Bake 10 to 12 minutes. Cool on wire racks.

JUDITH L. MCVAUGH

TIP ***After you chop the walnuts, place them in a strainer and shake over the sink to remove papery skin.***

Double Chocolate Treasures

PHOTO ON PAGE 128

MAKES:
About 5 dozen.

FREEZEWORTHY:
Yes, but cool completely first.

NOTES

A chocolate cookie studded with chocolate chips provides a double dose of goodness. The last-minute roll in confectioners' sugar makes this cookie that much better.

1 (12-ounce) package semisweet chocolate chips, divided use
½ cup (1 stick) unsalted butter, room temperature
¾ cup sugar
2 eggs
1 teaspoon vanilla
2 cups quick- or old-fashioned rolled oats
1½ cups all-purpose flour
2 teaspoons baking powder
¼ teaspoon salt
½ cup confectioners' sugar

Preheat oven to 350 degrees.

Melt 1 cup chocolate chips in heavy 2-quart saucepan over low heat. Stir until smooth; cool slightly.

In a mixing bowl, beat together butter and sugar until light and fluffy. Blend in eggs, vanilla and melted chocolate; set aside. In a separate bowl, combine oats, flour, baking powder and salt. Add to chocolate mixture; stir well. Stir in remaining chocolate chips. Shape dough into 1-inch balls and roll in confectioners' sugar, coating heavily.

Place on ungreased cookie sheet and bake 10 to 12 minutes. Remove from oven and cool 1 minute; remove cookies to wire rack to cool completely. Store in airtight container.

JOANNE CHERRY

White Chocolate Orange Dreams

PHOTO ON PAGE 130

MAKES:
3½ dozen.

FREEZEWORTHY:
Yes, but cool completely first.

NOTES

Chocolate and orange are natural pairings, and this cookie gets a double dose of citrus from orange zest and extract. Substitute semisweet chocolate chips for the white chocolate for a tasty variation.

1 cup (2 sticks) unsalted butter, room temperature
⅔ cup light brown sugar, firmly packed
½ cup granulated sugar
1 large egg
1 tablespoon grated orange zest
2 teaspoons orange extract
2 ¼ cups all-purpose flour
¾ teaspoon baking soda
½ teaspoon salt
2 cups white chocolate morsels

Preheat oven to 350 degrees.

Beat butter and sugars in a mixing bowl with an electric mixer at medium speed until creamy. Add egg, orange zest and extract, beating until blended. Set aside.

Combine flour, baking soda and salt in a separate bowl. Gradually add these dry ingredients to the butter mixture, beating just until blended after each addition. Stir in white chocolate morsels. Drop dough by rounded tablespoonsful onto ungreased baking sheets.

Bake for 10 to 12 minutes or until edges are lightly browned. Cool on baking sheets 2 minutes. Remove to wire racks to cool completely.

GAYLE HACKBARTH

TIP ! *Many recipes call for citrus fruit zest. To save time, use a Microplane®, which shaves off the flavorful colored skin in fine ribbons. Use only the colored skin and as little of the bitter white pith as possible*

Chocolate Nut Rolls

PHOTO ON PAGE 129

MAKES:
About 4 dozen.

FREEZEWORTHY:
Yes, but cool completely first.

NOTES

This cookie is made with a tender dough studded with mini-chocolate chips and then is given another hit in a chocolaty dip before being sprinkled with nuts. Leave out the nuts if you wish and you've still got a heck of a cookie.

2¼ cups sifted all-purpose flour
½ teaspoon salt
¾ cup softened margarine
¾ cup sugar
1 egg
1½ teaspoons vanilla
1 (6-ounce) package mini-chocolate chips

CHOCOLATE DIP:
1 (12-ounce) package chocolate chips
¼ cup margarine
2 cups chopped walnuts

Preheat oven to 350 degrees.

Sift flour and salt into a large mixing bowl. In another bowl, beat together margarine, sugar, egg and vanilla till blended. Add sifted flour and mini-chocolate chips to margarine mixture; combine well. Shape dough into 2-inch-by-½-inch logs on a lightly floured surface. Bake on ungreased cookie sheets for 12 to 15 minutes or until cookies are set. Cool on wire rack.

Melt chocolate chips and margarine in a double boiler. Dip ends of cookies (which should be cooled to room temperature) into chocolate and then into chopped walnuts. Place on waxed paper until the chocolate sets. Store in airtight container.

KIM SULLIVAN

Chipper Doodles

PHOTO ON PAGE 127

MAKES: About 2 dozen.

FREEZEWORTHY: Yes, but cool completely first.

NOTES

The classic snickerdoodle gets decidedly more decadent with the addition of chocolate chips. Use a combination of milk chocolate and semisweet for a ramped up version.

2½ cups all-purpose flour
2 teaspoons cream of tartar
1 teaspoon baking soda
¼ teaspoon salt
1 cup (2 sticks) unsalted butter, room temperature
½ cup light brown sugar
1 cup plus 2 tablespoons granulated sugar, divided use
2 eggs
1 (12-ounce) package chocolate chips
4 teaspoons ground cinnamon

Sift the flour, cream of tartar, baking soda and salt into a mixing bowl and set aside.

In a stand mixer, cream butter and brown sugar and 1 cup of the granulated sugar on medium speed until light and fluffy. Add the eggs and mix until combined. Add the flour mixture, and beat on low just until combined. Gently stir in chocolate chips.

Chill dough for about 30 minutes.

About 10 minutes before baking, preheat oven to 350 degrees.

Combine cinnamon and sugar in a small bowl.

Roll tablespoon-sized balls of dough in the cinnamon sugar and place on parchment-lined cookie sheets about 3 inches apart. Bake for 8 to 10 minutes. Cool cookies on wire racks.

Double Chocolate Chip Cookies

PHOTO ON PAGE 130

MAKES:
About 3 dozen.

FREEZEWORTHY:
Yes, but cool completely first.

NOTES

What's not to like? The addition of white chocolate chips lends more flavor and an appealing presentation.

2½ cups sifted all-purpose flour
1 scant teaspoon baking soda
2 teaspoons salt
¾ cup granulated sugar
¾ cup packed light brown sugar
1 cup (2 sticks) unsalted butter, room temperature
2 jumbo eggs
1 tablespoon vanilla
12 ounces semisweet or milk chocolate chips
6 ounces white chocolate chips
1 cup pecan pieces (optional)

Preheat oven to 350 degrees.

Sift flour with baking soda and salt in a large mixing bowl. Set aside.

Combine granulated and brown sugars with the butter and beat on highest speed of an electric mixer until creamy. Scrape bowl several times during the mixing. Beat in eggs, one at a time. Scrape sides. Add vanilla.

Add flour mixture until blended. Scrape sides of the bowl as you work.

Stir in chocolate chips and nuts, if desired. Cover a baking sheet with parchment paper. Drop by tablespoonsful onto baking sheet, spacing batter 1 inch apart. Flatten each cookie slightly with the palm of your hand.

Bake 8 to 10 minutes, depending on your choice of soft or crisp cookies. Cool completely before stacking in an airtight container.

VALERIE HART

cookielicious™

AUNTIE'S GINGERSNAPS

PAGE 30

COCONUT KRISPIES DROPS

PAGE 36

ANYTIME!

KEY LIME COOLERS

PAGE 33

COCONUT OATMEAL COOKIES

PAGE 37

ROSEMARY SHORTBREAD

PAGE 18

FROSTED DATE DROPS

PAGE 21

TOFFEE SQUARES

PAGE 40

HONEY-ROASTED PEANUT CRISPS

PAGE 34

MOON COOKIES

PAGE 35

LEMON NUTMEG MELTAWAYS

PAGE 41

CREAM CHEESE ROLL-UPS

PAGE 42

BUTTER BRICKLE & PECAN COOKIES

PAGE 24

ANYTIME!

OATMEAL BOURBON COOKIES

PAGE 28

MOCHA MACADAMIA SHORTBREAD

PAGE 15

HONEY COOKIES

PAGE 39

BUFFALO COOKIES
PAGE 29

WHITE CHOCOLATE MACAROONS
PAGE 20

MACADAMIA SNOWBALLS
PAGE 26

APRICOT BARS
PAGE 16

NO ORDINARY OATMEAL COOKIES
PAGE 31

OATMEAL GINGERSNAPS

PAGE 25

HAWAIIAN DELIGHTS

PAGE 14

ANYTIME!

NUT-RIBBON STRIPS

PAGE 43

POTATO CHIP PECAN CRUNCH COOKIES

PAGE 22

GERMAN SPICE COOKIES

PAGE 19

LEMON COCONUT SNAPS

PAGE 32

TOFFEE CRISPS

PAGE 38

GLAZED APPLE COOKIES

PAGE 17

FROSTED CASHEW COOKIES

PAGE 23

CHUBBY HUBBY COOKIES

PAGE 27

HEAVENLY CREAM WAFERS

PAGE 69

AMARETTO BUTTER BALLS

PAGE 52

SHARING!

BEST-EVER BRICKLE

PAGE 60

CASHEW YUMMIES

PAGE 61

BRANDIED APRICOT CHEWS

PAGE 67

CHERRY CHEESECAKE BARS

PAGE 76

COOKIES D'ITALIA

PAGE 64

CHEWY PECAN BARS

PAGE 58

STRAWBERRY ALMOND BARS

PAGE 73

CHERRY CHOCOLATE STRIPES

PAGE 57

CORNMEAL LEMON COOKIES

PAGE 62

COFFEE TOFFEE BARS

PAGE 55

SHARING!

HAZELNUT CRINKLE COOKIES

PAGE 65

FROSTED MOLASSES SQUARES

PAGE 53

RASPBERRY SUGAR BARS

PAGE 70

PECAN PUFFS

PAGE 50

ORANGE CITRUS BARS

PAGE 75

BUTTER PECAN TURTLE BARS

PAGE 59

OATMEAL CARMELITA BARS

PAGE 71

CORNMEAL COOKIES WITH CURRANTS

PAGE 72

ORANGE DROP COOKIES

PAGE 51

PEACH STREUSEL BARS

PAGE 54

SHARING!

CREAM CHEESE & BASIL COOKIES

PAGE 56

PECAN PICK-UPS

PAGE 66

COCONUT JAM BARS

PAGE 74

LEMON RASPBERRY THUMBPRINTS

PAGE 63

PISTACHIO & CHERRY SNOWBALLS

PAGE 68

PEANUT BUTTER SANDWICH COOKIES

PAGE 49

PINEAPPLE SCOTCH BARS

PAGE 77

TIPSIES

PAGE 48

BLACK MOUNTAIN COOKIES

PAGE 85

CHOCOLATE YUM-YUMS

PAGE 88

CHOCOLATE!

CHOCOLATE COFFEE BATONS

PAGE 103

CHOCO-COCO PECAN CRISPS

PAGE 100

CHOCOLATE
CINS

PAGE 106

BUCKEYES
IN THE PAN

PAGE 84

CHOCOLATE
WALNUT PUFFS

PAGE 86

CHIPPER DOODLES

PAGE 110

FUDGY CITRUS COOKIES

PAGE 97

CHEWY CHOCOLATE ORANGE NUGGETS

PAGE 101

MINT CHOCOLATE COOKIES

PAGE 87

CHOCOLATE CRUNCH MORSELS

PAGE 95

CHOCOLATE!

TRIPLE CHOCOLATE HAZELNUT BISCOTTI

PAGE 89

DOUBLE CHOCOLATE TREASURES

PAGE 107

CHOCOLATE NUT ROLLS
PAGE 109

DEATH BY CHOCOLATE COOKIES
PAGE 104

WHITE CHOCOLATE CRANBERRY DROPS
PAGE 83

CHOCOLATE-MINT CRÈME COOKIES
PAGE 93

THIS LITTLE PIGGY HAD A COOKIE
PAGE 94

CHOCOLATE SNOWBALLS

PAGE 90

WHITE CHOCOLATE ORANGE DREAMS

PAGE 108

CHOCOLATE!

CARAMEL BARS

PAGE 98

DOUBLE CHOCOLATE CHIP COOKIES

PAGE 111

CHOCOLATE MACAROON MERINGUE BITES

PAGE 99

MOCHA TRUFFLE COOKIES

PAGE 102

CRUNCHY FUDGE BARS

PAGE 92

COCONUT CHOCOLATE CLUSTERS

PAGE 82

HOT CHOCOLATE BALLS

PAGE 96

TROPICAL WHITE CHOCOLATE COOKIES

PAGE 105

CRÈME DE MENTHE CHOCOLATE SQUARES

PAGE 91

FRUITY COOKIES
PAGE 177

BAILEY BONES (DOGGIE COOKIES)
PAGE 164

KIDS!

CHOCOLATE RAISIN OATIES
PAGE 173

O'HENRY BARS
PAGE 158

CHOCOLATE MARSHMALLOW SLICES

PAGE 172

LEMON SNOWFLAKES

PAGE 154

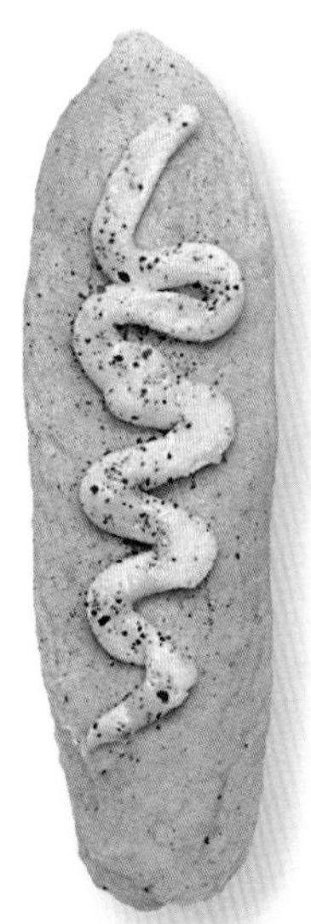

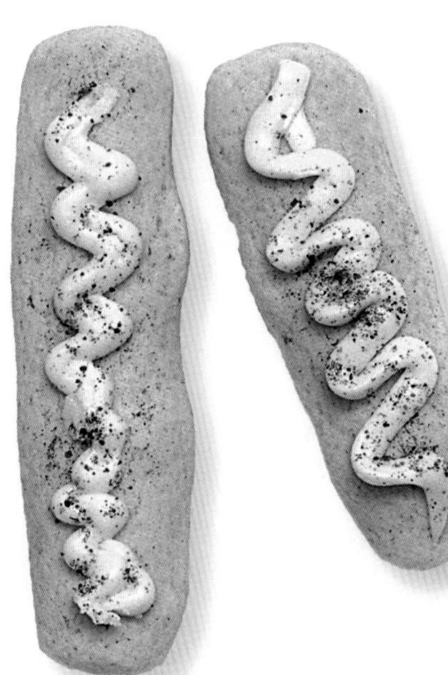

NUTMEG BUTTER FINGERS

PAGE 163

BUTTERSCOTCH CHIPPERS

PAGE 178

CHOCOLATE BON BON COOKIES

PAGE 169

PEACHY CROSTINI COOKIES
PAGE 153

RAISIN CRINKLES
PAGE 159

KIDS!

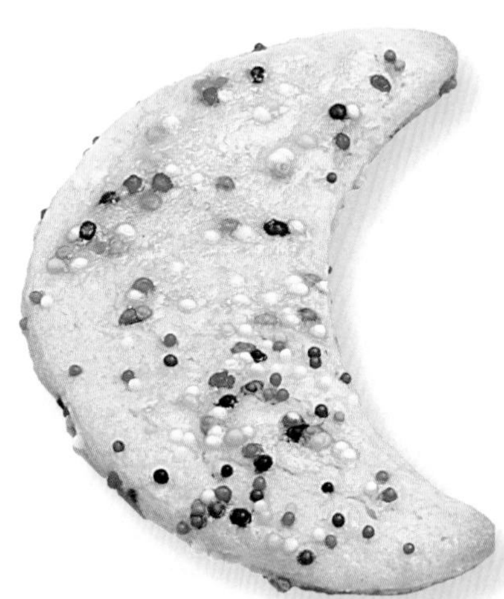

CREAM CHEESE SUGAR COOKIES
PAGE 174

PEANUT LOVER CHOCOLATE COOKIES
PAGE 165

MINI PEANUT BUTTER TREATS
PAGE 175

DOUBLE TROUBLE COOKIES

PAGE 151

SPIDER COOKIES

PAGE 162

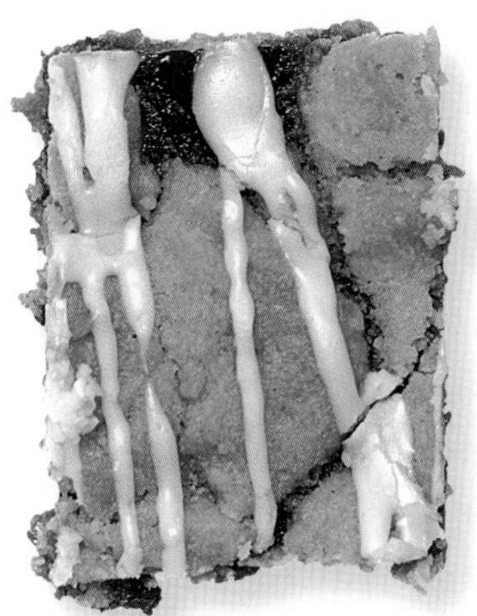

PEANUT BUTTER & JAM BARS

PAGE 161

MINT COOKIES

PAGE 156

WHITE CHOCOLATE DELIGHT

PAGE 160

PEANUT BUTTER BANANA COOKIES

PAGE 176

GUMDROP GEMS

PAGE 179

ROOT BEER COOKIES

PAGE 157

KIDS!

CHEWY ROLO® BROWNIES

PAGE 166

CHOCOLATE MINT SUGAR COOKIES

PAGE 168

CHOCOLATE CORN FLAKE COOKIES

PAGE 152

SNICKERS® COOKIES

PAGE 155

POLKA DOT COOKIES

PAGE 150

LICORICE SNAPS

PAGE 171

JOYFUL ALMOND BLONDIES

PAGE 170

ORANGE CREAMSICLE DROPS

PAGE 167

RETRO
JEWEL
COOKIES
PAGE 196

PEPPERMINT
PINWHEELS
PAGE 212

HOLIDAY!

YULETIDE
COOKIE BARS
PAGE 189

SITTING
PRETTIES
PAGE 202

CATHEDRAL COOKIES

PAGE 210

DIPPED GINGERSNAPS

PAGE 209

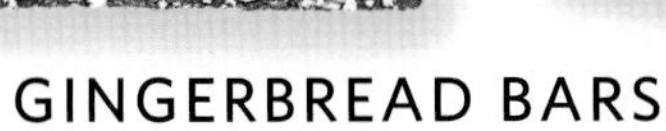

GINGERBREAD BARS

PAGE 203

CANDY CANE PUFFS

PAGE 208

CHERRY SQUARES

PAGE 199

MOLASSES CRINKLES

PAGE 194

PUMPKIN DROP COOKIES

PAGE 200

SNOW TOPPED MINT BARS

PAGE 198

HOLIDAY!

DATE-NUT KRISPIES

PAGE 184

CANDIED FRUIT SLICES

PAGE 204

SANTA'S SPECIAL SQUARES

PAGE 186

CANDY CANE GINGERSNAPS

PAGE 195

WHITE CHRISTMAS SHORTBREAD

PAGE 201

HOLIDAY RAISIN WALNUT BARS

PAGE 191

PEPPERMINT WANDS

PAGE 205

NUTTY CHERRY NO-BAKES

PAGE 188

GRAND MARNIER® WREATHS
PAGE 193

CHERRY NUT SLICES
PAGE 213

HOLIDAY!

WALNUT & SOUR CREAM COOKIES
PAGE 185

ORANGE SPICE GEMS
PAGE 207

SANTA'S WHISKERS
PAGE 206

SNOWBALL SURPRISES

PAGE 190

CRANBERRY CHERRY PINWHEELS

PAGE 187

PEPPERMINT FUDGIES

PAGE 197

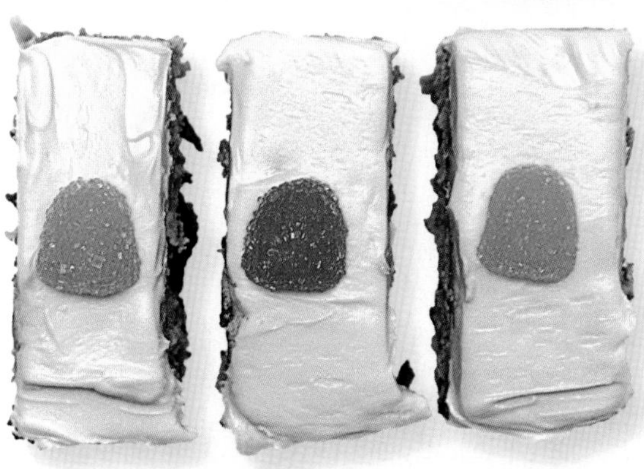

GUMDROP BARS

PAGE 192

CRANBERRY ORANGE COOKIES

PAGE 211

equivalent measurements

LIQUID MEASURES

1 gallon = 4 quarts = 8 pint = 16 cups = 128 fluid ounces

½ gallon = 2 quarts = 4 pints = 8 cups = 64 fluid ounces

¼ gallon = 1 quart = 2 pints = 4 cups = 32 fluid ounces

½ quart = 1 pint = 2 cups = 16 fluid ounces

¼ quart = ½ pint = 1 cup = 8 fluid ounces

4 quarts = 1 gallon

DRY MEASURES

1 cup = 16 tablespoons = 48 teaspoons = 250ml

¾ cup = 12 tablespoons = 36 teaspoons = 175ml

⅔ cup = 10⅔ tablespoons = 32 teaspoons = 150ml

½ cup = 8 tablespoons = 24 teaspoons = 125ml

⅓ cup = 5⅓ tablespoons = 16 teaspoons = 75ml

¼ cup = 4 tablespoons = 12 teaspoons = 50ml

⅛ cup = 2 tablespoons = 6 teaspoons = 30ml

1 tablespoon = 3 teaspoons = 15ml

16 ounces = 1 pound

Dash or pinch = less than ⅛ teaspoon

CHAPTER 4

KIDS

SWEETS FOR YOUNGSTERS TO BAKE OR TO ENJOY WITH A GLASS OF MILK

Cracking eggs and using the hand mixer are often the first kitchen techniques mastered by children — in the name of homemade chocolate chip cookies!

Children are good kitchen helpers, though it's important for the adult on duty to understand their skill level. Stirring and measuring can be handled by all ages, but using knives and removing hot baking sheets from the oven should be reserved for older children.

Besides providing quality together time, baking cookies, and cooking in general, can help children hone their math and reading skills. They will hardly know they're in "school" when the results of their work are warm cookies made with lots of loving.

Many of the cookies in this chapter are simple enough for novice bakers. Several are even no-bakes. Some require more skill, but they include favorite childhood flavors.

KIDS! COOKIES

Polka Dot Cookies

PHOTO ON PAGE 137

MAKES:
4 dozen.

FREEZEWORTHY:
Yes, but cool completely first.

How much easier can cookie baking get? Start with a brownie mix and add white chocolate chips to make the festive polka dots.

1 (21.2-ounce) package fudge brownie mix
½ cup vegetable oil
2 large eggs
1 cup white chocolate morsels or vanilla-milk chocolate morsels

Preheat oven to 350 degrees.

Combine first three ingredients, stirring well. Stir in morsels. Drop dough by rounded teaspoonful about 2 inches apart onto ungreased baking sheets. Bake for 10 minutes. Cool cookies on pan 2 minutes; remove to wire racks to cool completely.

FLORENCE TIRABASSI

TIP *To keep cookies from spreading too much, use butter that's just soft enough to cream with sugar, but not so warm that it melts the moment it hits the oven. Butter is ready when it yields to slight pressure, and depending on the temperature of your house, this could take an hour sitting on the counter.*

NOTES

Double Trouble Cookies

PHOTO ON PAGE 135

MAKES:
About 3 dozen.

FREEZEWORTHY:
Yes, but cool completely first.

NOTES

Save this recipe for a special gathering of kids. The combo is irresistible: half peanut butter, half chocolate and all good, especially with the addition of chocolate-coated peanut butter candy.

2½ cups unbleached all-purpose flour, plus an additional ¼ cup
1 teaspoon baking soda
¾ teaspoon salt
½ cup (1 stick) unsalted butter, room temperature
⅓ cup creamy peanut butter
¾ cup granulated sugar
¾ cup packed brown sugar
2 large eggs
2 teaspoons vanilla
1 cup peanut butter M&M's®
¼ cup unsweetened cocoa powder

Sift together in a medium size bowl, 2½ cups flour, baking soda and salt. Set aside.

Beat together until creamy, butter, peanut butter and sugars in a large bowl, using an electric mixer set on medium speed, about 2 minutes. Beat in eggs and vanilla until well combined. Reduce mixer speed to low and gradually beat in flour mixture until combined.

Divide dough into two bowls. In one bowl, beat in additional ¼ cup flour until combined then stir in peanut butter M&M's®. In second bowl, beat in cocoa powder until combined. Lightly cover both doughs and chill in the refrigerator until firm, about 15 minutes.

Shape dough into two logs about 2-by-12-inches and wrap in separate pieces of plastic wrap; chill for 1 hour.

Remove cookie dough logs from refrigerator and cut in half lengthwise. Pair half of peanut butter dough log with chocolate dough half. Repeat to make a second log. Rewrap each separately and chill for another hour or overnight.

Preheat oven to 350 degrees and line baking sheets with parchment paper.

Slice logs into ⅓-inch thick rounds, place on cookie sheets, and bake for 10 to 12 minutes, or until golden brown around edges. Cool 1 minute before transferring to wire racks to cool completely.

JANET K. KEELER

Chocolate Corn Flake Cookies

PHOTO ON PAGE 136

MAKES: About 4 dozen.

FREEZEWORTHY: No. The corn flakes will get soggy when thawed.

NOTES

Nothing could be simpler than this recipe. Have the kids wash their hands before they plunge them into this silly dough of chocolate and corn flakes. There is no baking involved, so the recipe is that much better for young helpers.

2 pounds milk chocolate
2 squares unsweetened baking chocolate
Large box corn flakes

Melt both chocolates in a double boiler and stir in as much of the corn flakes as possible, making sure that they are coated well.

Drop by large, compact tablespoonsful onto a cookie sheet that's lined with wax paper. Refrigerate until set. Store in the refrigerator.

SUSAN HUSSEY

TIP *To make a simple chocolate cookie more appealing to sophisticated tastes, swap semi-sweet or milk chocolate for bittersweet, dark or citrus-tinged chocolate.*

Peachy Crostini Cookies

PHOTO ON PAGE 134

MAKES:
2 dozen.

FREEZEWORTHY:
Not recommended.

NOTES

Consider these faux-fancy cookies for a children's tea party. Change up the flavor with any preserves you want.

½ cup granulated sugar
5 tablespoons unsalted butter, room temperature
1½ teaspoons vanilla
1 large egg
1 cup all-purpose flour
2 tablespoons cornstarch
¼ teaspoon baking powder
¼ teaspoon salt
Cooking spray
⅓ cup peach preserves

ICING:
½ cup confectioners' sugar
2 teaspoons fresh lemon juice
¼ teaspoon vanilla

Preheat oven to 375 degrees.

Beat granulated sugar and butter with a mixer at medium speed until well-blended (about 5 minutes). Add 1½ teaspoons vanilla and egg; beat well. Set aside.

Lightly spoon flour into a dry measuring cup; level with a knife.

Combine flour, cornstarch, baking powder and salt in a large mixing bowl, stirring well with a whisk. Add flour mixture to sugar mixture, stirring until well-blended. (Dough will be stiff.)

Turn dough out onto a lightly floured surface. Divide dough in half. Roll each portion into a 12-inch log. Place logs 3 inches apart on a baking sheet coated with cooking spray. Form a ½-inch-deep indentation down the length of each log using an index finger or end of a wooden spoon. Spoon preserves into the center. Bake for 20 minutes or until lightly browned. Remove logs to a cutting board.

Combine confectioners' sugar, lemon juice and vanilla; stir well with a whisk. Drizzle sugar mixture over warm logs. Immediately cut each log diagonally into 12 slices. (Do not separate slices.) Cool 10 minutes; separate slices. Transfer slices to wire racks. Cool completely.

Lemon Snowflakes

PHOTO ON PAGE 133

MAKES:
3 to 4 dozen.

FREEZEWORTHY:
So-so results. This is a soft cookie that will become softer when thawed.

NOTES

For even more lemon flavor, add ¼ teaspoon of lemon extract. Consider this recipe your template for experimentation with chocolate, vanilla, spice or even carrot cake mixes. It is easy enough for small children to help.

1 (18-ounce) box lemon cake mix
1 (8-ounce) tub of non-dairy whipped topping
1 egg
Confectioners' sugar

Preheat oven to 350 degrees.

Combine cake mix, whipped topping and egg in a mixing bowl, beating or stirring until blended. (Batter will be very sticky.) Drop by teaspoonsful into confectioners' sugar and roll lightly to coat. Place on greased cookie sheet. Bake for 10 to 12 minutes, or until lightly browned.

Variations: Use white cake mix with 1 teaspoon almond flavoring. Add coconut to any variation.

JANICE CHANDLER

TIP *Cool cookie sheets between batches; better yet, buy two or three sheets. Don't grease the cookie sheet unless the recipe calls for it or cookies may spread and brown too quickly around the edges.*

Snickers® Cookies

PHOTO ON PAGE 137

MAKES:
About 5 dozen.

FREEZEWORTHY:
Yes, but cool completely first and glaze after they are thawed.

NOTES

This is a shameful nod to my favorite candy bar. Look for the tiniest size Snickers® bars you can find and the dough will wrap nicely around them.

1 cup (2 sticks) unsalted butter, room temperature
1 cup creamy peanut butter
1 cup sugar
1 cup light brown sugar, firmly packed
2 eggs
2 teaspoons vanilla
3 cups all-purpose flour
1 teaspoon baking soda
1 teaspoon baking powder
2 bags mini Snickers® candy bars

GLAZE:
1 cup confectioners' sugar
2 tablespoons unsweetened cocoa
1 tablespoon milk

Preheat oven to 350 degrees.

Cream butter, peanut butter, sugars in a large mixing bowl. Add eggs and vanilla; set aside. Combine flour, baking soda and baking powder. Add to peanut butter mixture a little at a time mixing thoroughly after each addition. Batter will be greasy and soft.

Take 1 rounded teaspoon of dough and flatten into round shape in the palm of your hand. Place Snickers® bar in center and fold dough around it. Roll in your palms to form a smooth ball (make sure Snickers® is covered or it will leak out during baking).

Place on ungreased cookie sheet and bake for 10 to 12 minutes or until edges are slightly golden. Remove from cookie sheet and cool.

To make glaze, mix confectioners' sugar, cocoa and milk together. Add additional milk as needed to thin mixture so it can be drizzled from a spoon. Drizzle tops of cookies with chocolate glaze.

CHRIS ALES

Mint Cookies

PHOTO ON PAGE 135

MAKES:
About 20.

FREEZEWORTHY:
Yes, but cool completely first.

NOTES

Instead of nuts, use chocolate jimmies or sprinkles to decorate the cookies. Children will be delighted when they find the mint candy surprise inside.

1 (18-ounce) package refrigerated sugar cookie dough
20 to 25 chocolate mints, such as Andes®
1 egg white, lightly beaten
¼ chopped pecans (optional)

Preheat oven to 350 degrees.

Slice packaged cookie dough into ¼-inch rounds. Place one slice on greased cookie sheet and top with mint. Cover with another slice of cookie and lightly press edges together. Brush with egg white and sprinkle with chopped nuts. Press nuts into dough, if using.

Continue working placing each cookie about 2 inches apart from the others. Bake for 10 to 12 minutes.

PHYLLIS VAN DIVER

TIP *Don't use vegetable oil for greasing baking sheets. The oil will burn and make cleanup difficult. If you aren't using parchment paper, grease sheets with vegetable shortening or unsalted butter.*

Root Beer Cookies

PHOTO ON PAGE 136

MAKES:
About 3 dozen.

FREEZEWORTHY:
No. Glaze gets gummy and soft cookies become even softer.

NOTES

I've fallen hard for this cookie and so will the root beer lovers in your house. The soda flavor is subtle and you may have to hunt for the extract. Sometimes it's called root beer concentrate. Seek it out. You — and your children — won't be disappointed.

1 cup brown sugar, firmly packed
½ cup (1 stick) unsalted butter, room temperature
1 egg
¼ cup buttermilk
1 teaspoon root beer extract
1¾ cups all-purpose flour
½ teaspoon baking soda
½ teaspoon salt

GLAZE:
2 cups confectioners' sugar
⅓ cup butter
1½ teaspoons root beer extract
2 tablespoons hot water

Mix together in a large bowl, brown sugar, butter, egg, buttermilk and root beer extract. Add flour, baking soda and salt; mix well. Chill dough for 1 hour.

About 10 minutes before baking, preheat oven to 350 degrees.

Using a small (about two teaspoons) ice cream scoop for uniform size, drop dough 2 inches apart onto greased cookie sheet. Bake for 9 to 11 minutes. Cool and top with glaze.

To make the glaze, mix together the confectioners' sugar, butter, root beer extract and hot water. Stir until well combined; spread over cookies.

MARY-ANN JANSSEN

O'Henry Bars

PHOTO ON PAGE 132

MAKES:
3 dozen bars.

FREEZEWORTHY:
No, but they can be made days ahead of time since they keep well the refrigerator.

Fans of the peanut butter candy bar will eat these up. They are no-bakes, too, and easy for young cooks to make.

½ cup (1 stick) unsalted butter
¼ cup light Karo® syrup
½ cup packed light brown sugar
2 cups quick- or old-fashioned oats, uncooked
½ cup semisweet chocolate chips
½ cup crunchy peanut butter

Melt butter in microwave-safe 8-inch square glass dish. Remove; mix in corn syrup and brown sugar. Stir in oats. Microwave on full power until bubbly, 3 to 4 minutes.

In separate microwave-safe bowl, melt chocolate chips and peanut butter for about 1 minute on medium setting. Stir and pour over hot mixture. Refrigerate until firm; cut into bars.

KAREN HARAM

NOTES

TIP ***Most recipes call for brown sugar to be firmly packed when measured. The added molasses makes the sugar thicker. Firmly packing it when measuring provides all the sweetness needed for the recipe.***

Raisin Crinkles

PHOTO ON PAGE 134

MAKES:
About 4 dozen.

FREEZEWORTHY:
Yes, but cool completely first.

NOTES

If you've got a wee one in the house, you just may have the jars of prune baby food that's used to sweeten this wholesome cookie. You could experiment with other flavors, but the prune gives a depth that pears and peaches probably won't.

2¼ cups all-purpose flour
1 teaspoon baking soda
1 teaspoon cinnamon
1 teaspoon ground ginger
1 teaspoon ground cloves
1 cup firmly packed brown sugar
2 (2.5 ounce each) jars prune baby food
¼ cup molasses
1 egg
1 cup raisins (soaked in boiling water for about 1 hour, then drained and blotted with paper towel)
Granulated sugar

Sift together flour, baking soda, cinnamon, ginger and cloves into a medium-size bowl. Set aside. Beat together in a large bowl, brown sugar, baby food, molasses and egg until well blended. Stir dry ingredients into creamed mixture until well blended. Stir in raisins. Cover and refrigerate at least one hour or overnight.

About 10 minutes before baking, preheat oven to 375 degrees.
Spray cookie sheets lightly with vegetable cooking spray and set aside.

Shape dough into 1-inch balls and roll in granulated sugar. Place on cookie sheet about 3 inches apart. Bake for 10 to 12 minutes or until set and tops have crinkled. Store in air tight container.

DONNA GROVE

White Chocolate Delight

PHOTO ON PAGE 135

MAKES:
About 3 dozen.

FREEZEWORTHY:
No, cereal will become soggy.

Shake your cereal boxes to see if you've got enough at the bottom to make these cookie confections. Kids of all ages can easily help.

1 pound white chocolate
1 cup Cap'n Crunch® peanut butter cereal
1 cup Rice Krispies®
1 cup miniature marshmallows
1 (12-ounce) jar dry roasted peanuts, optional

Melt chocolate in double boiler over low heat. Do not let boil.

Mix together cereal, marshmallows and peanuts, if using. Gently stir into melted chocolate, taking care not to break up cereal. Drop by rounded teaspoonsful onto cookie sheets lined with wax paper. Place in freezer for a few minutes to harden, then refrigerate until set.

KATHERINE CORTINA

NOTES

TIP *The cereal aisle is an unexpected place to look for cookie ingredients. Nearly any cereal can be used in a no-bake recipe or add crunch to a simple chocolate chip, peanut butter or sugar cookie.*

Peanut Butter & Jam Bars

PHOTO ON PAGE 135

MAKES: 3 dozen.

FREEZEWORTHY: No.

NOTES

Make this for a special occasion like a child's party. Older kids can help, but mostly they'll just want to eat this variation on a favorite childhood sandwich.

½ cup sugar
½ cup brown sugar
½ cup (1 stick) unsalted butter, room temperature
½ cup peanut butter
1 egg
1¼ cup all-purpose flour
¾ teaspoon baking soda
½ teaspoon baking powder
½ cup raspberry jam

GLAZE:
2 tablespoons unsalted butter
1 cup confectioners' sugar
1 teaspoon vanilla
1 to 2 tablespoons hot water

Preheat oven to 350 degrees.

Cream sugars, butter, peanut butter and egg in a large mixing bowl. Stir in flour, baking soda and baking powder, and mix well. Reserve 1 cup dough. Press remaining dough into ungreased 13-inch-by-9-inch pan. Spread with jam, then crumble reserved dough and sprinkle over jam. Bake until golden brown (approximately 20 minutes). Cool while preparing glaze.

To make the glaze, heat butter over low heat. Mix in confectioners' sugar and vanilla. Beat in hot water, 1 teaspoon at a time, till smooth. Drizzle glaze over top and cut into 2-inch-by-1½-inch bars.

DOLORES A. HAASE

Spider Cookies

PHOTO ON PAGE 135

MAKES: About 2 dozen.

FREEZEWORTHY: No, noodles will become soggy.

NOTES

This cookie provides a good way to use up leftover chow mein noodles. A fun project for when your child has friends over. Good and messy.

6 ounces chocolate chips
6 ounces butterscotch chips
3 ounces crunchy Chinese chow mein noodles.

Place chocolate and butterscotch chips in a 2-quart saucepan over medium heat. Stir until chips are melted. Remove from heat and add chow mein noodles, turning over gently until all are coated. Drop in tablespoon-size heaps on wax paper-lined cookie tray.

Refrigerate until set (overnight is best).

TIP ***Wrap trays loosely with plastic or foil when chilling no-bake cookies overnight. This prevents other refrigerator odors from spoiling your sweet treats.***

Nutmeg Butter Fingers

PHOTO ON PAGE 133

MAKES:
4 to 5 dozen.

FREEZEWORTHY:
No, unless they are frozen before the frosting is added.

NOTES

Older children may have fun rolling the dough in finger-like shapes. It's easier to frost these cookies if you put the icing in a plastic bag, snip a corner and drizzle the icing over the cookies.

1 cup (2 sticks) unsalted butter, room temperature
¾ cup sugar
1 egg
2 teaspoons vanilla
3 cups sifted all-purpose flour
¾ teaspoon ground nutmeg

ICING:
½ cup (1 stick) unsalted butter, room temperature
1 teaspoon vanilla
2 cups confectioners' sugar
2½ tablespoons half-and-half
Ground nutmeg

Preheat oven to 350 degrees.

Make cookies by creaming together butter and sugar gradually, beating until light and fluffy. Add egg and vanilla. Mix well.

Sift flour and nutmeg and add to egg mixture. Blend well. Pinch off bits of dough and roll into cookies the size of a little finger.

Place on greased cookie sheets and bake 13 to 15 minutes, until set and lightly browned. Cool.

To make icing, cream butter, and then add vanilla. Add confectioners' sugar and beat until smooth. Add half-and-half, and beat again.

Frost cooled cookies and sprinkle with nutmeg.

CAROL BICKFORD

Bailey Bones (Doggie Cookies)

PHOTO ON PAGE 132

MAKES:
About 3 dozen.

FREEZEWORTHY:
Yes, but they'll keep just fine in an air-tight container for a few weeks.

NOTES

These really are for dogs, but I sampled them anyway. Not bad. They tasted a little like Triscuit® crackers, and later, I did notice a strong urge to scratch behind my ears.

1¼ cup whole wheat flour
½ cup quick-cooking rolled oats
1 egg, slightly beaten
½ cup all-purpose flour
1 teaspoon sugar
¾ cup powdered milk
¼ cup yellow cornmeal
½ cup hot water
⅓ cup vegetable oil
1 tablespoon chicken or beef bouillon granules

Preheat oven to 350 degrees.

Mix all ingredients in a large bowl until well blended. Roll out on floured board to a ¼-inch thickness. Cut out treats with bone-shaped cookie cutter. Bake 15 to 20 minutes or until dry.

MARCIA MANDERVILLE

TIP *If your cookie dough is dry and crumbling, add 1 to 2 tablespoons of milk or cream. Work this into the dough by hand or with a wooden spoon rather than a mixer.*

Peanut Lover Chocolate Cookies

PHOTO ON PAGE 134

MAKES:
About 4 dozen.

FREEZEWORTHY:
Yes, but cool completely first.

NOTES

I am a peanut lover so this is one of my favorite cookies. It's a simple spin on a chocolate chip cookie but the salted peanuts take it to a whole new place. Nutty kids will love it too.

2 ⅓ cups all-purpose flour
1½ teaspoons baking soda
1 teaspoon baking powder
1 teaspoon salt
1 cup (2 sticks) unsalted butter, room temperature
1 cup light brown sugar
1 cup granulated sugar
2 large eggs
1 teaspoon vanilla
1⅓ cups creamy peanut butter
1 (8-ounce) package semisweet chocolate chunks
½ cup salted peanuts

Preheat the oven to 350 degrees.

In a medium bowl, combine the flour, baking soda, baking powder and salt. Set aside.

Beat the butter with the sugars until fluffy in a large bowl, using an electric mixer. Add the eggs and vanilla and beat at low speed until blended. Add the peanut butter and beat until combined. Beat in the dry ingredients just until incorporated. Fold in the chocolate chunks and peanuts.

Drop by 2 tablespoon-size scoops on parchment-lined baking sheets, 2 inches apart. Bake for 10 to 12 minutes. Cool on wire racks.

JANET K. KEELER

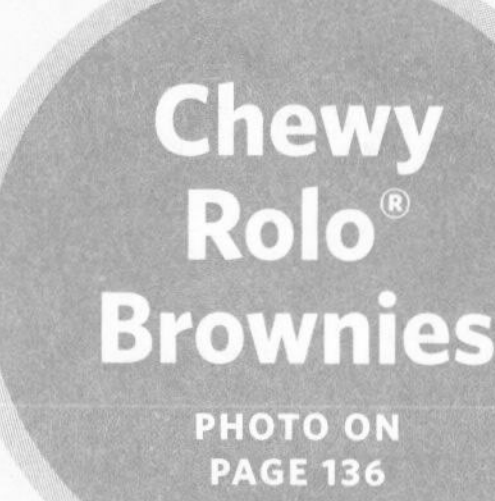

Chewy Rolo® Brownies

PHOTO ON PAGE 136

MAKES:
3 dozen squares.

FREEZEWORTHY:
No.

Make sure you let the bars cool before eating; otherwise the molten candy could burn the mouth just like a hot pizza bitten too soon.

36 Rolo® candies, unwrapped
½ cup unsalted butter
1 (18-ounce) yellow cake mix
½ cup chopped nuts, optional
1 (12-ounce) can evaporated milk (not condensed milk)

Preheat oven to 350 degrees. Grease a 9-inch-by-13-inch pan. Set aside.

Cut Rolo® pieces in half crosswise; set aside. Melt butter in microwave; set aside.

Combine cake mix and nuts. Stir in melted butter and evaporated milk until well blended. Spread half of mixture in prepared pan. Bake for 15 minutes. Remove from oven and immediately place candy onto warm crust.

Drop remaining batter by teaspoonsful evenly over candy in pan. Do not spread. Bake for 25 to 30 minutes until lightly browned. Cool completely before cutting.

JEANNE GLEASON

NOTES

TIP *Make cookies the same size and shape so they will finish baking at the same time.*

Orange Creamsicle Drops

PHOTO ON PAGE 137

MAKES:
About 2½ dozen.

FREEZEWORTHY:
Yes, but cool completely first.

NOTES

The flavors that taste great frozen and on a stick also translate to a tempting cookie. The kids will almost believe they've gotten something from the ice cream truck. This recipe is easy enough for them to help bake it.

1¾ cups all-purpose flour
1 package (.15-ounce) unsweetened orange drink mix, such as Kool-Aid®
½ teaspoon baking soda
½ teaspoon baking powder
½ cup (1 stick) unsalted butter, room temperature
1 cup sugar
2 eggs
1 teaspoon orange extract
1¼ cups white baking chips

Preheat oven to 350 degrees.

Combine flour, drink mix, baking soda and baking powder in a bowl and set aside.

Cream together softened butter and sugar. Add eggs and orange extract and beat until blended.

Add flour mixture all at once and mix on low speed until just blended. Stir in white baking chips by hand.

Drop rounded tablespoons of dough on lightly greased cookie sheet. Bake for about 10 minutes. Cookies should be slightly under baked when they come out of the oven. Do not wait for edges to brown. Immediately remove to rack to cool.

NANCY CRUZ

Chocolate Mint Sugar Cookies

PHOTO ON PAGE 136

MAKES:
4 dozen.

FREEZEWORTHY:
Yes, both the dough and the cooled, baked cookies.

NOTES

This recipe is an Internet favorite and may just remind you of a Girl Scout cookie. If you can't find the swirled chips, use all chocolate and add 1 teaspoon of peppermint extract to the dough. The beauty here is that the dough can be shaped and frozen, then baked when you feel the need for a few fresh-baked cookies.

½ cup (1 stick) butter, cut into cubes
1 (17.5-ounce) package sugar cookie mix
1 egg, beaten
1 (10-ounce) package semisweet chocolate-mint swirled morsels

Place butter in a large microwave-safe mixing bowl. Heat on high until butter is melted, about 30 to 45 seconds. Add sugar cookie mix, egg, and chocolate mint morsels; mix well. Form dough into 48 approximately 1-inch size balls.

The cookie dough balls can be placed in a covered container and frozen. When ready to bake cookies, heat oven to 350 degrees. Take out desired number of cookie dough balls and place on large cookie sheet. Bake for about 10 minutes or until cookies are lightly brown. Cookie dough balls that are not frozen or that are thawed will take only about 7 minutes to bake until cookies are lightly brown.

KATHY FLAREAU

TIP ***For chewy cookies, bake dough for the least amount of time specified in the recipe. The longer baking time will yield crisper cookies.***

Chocolate Bon Bon Cookies

PHOTO ON PAGE 133

MAKES:
4 dozen.

FREEZEWORTHY:
Yes, but cool completely first.

NOTES

Bon Bons are a personal favorite. I've been making them since my son was in grade school. I usually bake a few batches and freeze a lot. They're so good he eats them frozen despite my warnings about cracking a tooth. Shaping them can be a tricky for small hands so plan on making a batch for the kids rather than with them.

1 (6-square) package white baking chocolate
1½ packages (12 squares) semisweet baking chocolate
¼ cup (½ stick) unsalted butter
1 (14-ounce) can sweetened condensed milk
1 teaspoon vanilla
2 cups all-purpose flour
½ cup finely chopped walnuts

Preheat oven to 350 degrees.

Chop each white chocolate square into 8 chunks; set aside.

Microwave semisweet chocolate and butter in large microwaveable bowl on high 2 minutes, or until butter is melted, stirring after 30 seconds. Stir until chocolate is completely melted. Blend in milk and vanilla. Add flour and walnuts; mix well (dough will be stiff).

Shape 1 level tablespoonful of dough around each white chocolate chunk, fully enclosing white chocolate. Place, 1 inch apart, on ungreased baking sheets.

Bake 6 to 8 minutes or until soft and shiny (cookies will firm as they cool). Remove to wire racks to cool completely.

LINDA SIEDLE

Joyful Almond Blondies

PHOTO ON PAGE 137

MAKES:
About 20 to 25 squares.

FREEZEWORTHY:
Not recommended.

NOTES

Many popular candies are now made in pieces and they lend themselves to baking. Who wouldn't want their favorite candy in a cookie? The chocolate, almond and coconut mixture of Almond Joy® blends quite well into this easy blondies recipe.

½ cup (1 stick) unsalted butter, melted
1 cup brown sugar
1 egg
1 teaspoon vanilla
¼ teaspoon salt
½ teaspoon baking powder
1 cup all-purpose flour
1 cup Almond Joy® pieces candy

Preheat oven to 350 degrees.

Mix melted butter into brown sugar in a medium mixing bowl; beat until smooth. Beat in egg and then vanilla. Add salt, baking powder and flour, mix until incorporated. Fold in Almond Joy® candy pieces.

Pour mixture into a greased 8-inch pan. Bake for 20 to 25 minutes or until blondies are set in the middle.

JANET K. KEELER

TIP *Bars and squares are done when the sides shrink from the pan or the top springs back lightly when touched.*

Licorice Snaps

PHOTO ON PAGE 137

MAKES: 3 to 4 dozen.

FREEZEWORTHY: Yes, but cool completely first.

NOTES

If you've got a child who loves licorice, then she'll love this cookie. And guess what? The adults will adore it, too. As nearly always, the nuts are optional in this recipe.

2½ cups all-purpose flour
1 teaspoon baking soda
½ teaspoon salt
½ teaspoon ground cloves
½ teaspoon cinnamon
1 cup (2 sticks) unsalted butter, room temperature
1 cup sugar
1 cup light brown sugar, firmly packed
1 egg
1 tablespoon anise seeds
½ cup chopped pecans (optional)

Combine flour, baking soda, salt, cloves and cinnamon in a large mixing bowl; set aside.

Cream butter and sugars in a large mixing bowl. Add egg; beat until blended. Gradually add flour mixture until well blended. Stir in anise seeds and pecans. Divide dough in half and shape into two 10-inch logs. Wrap in wax paper and chill for at least 1 hour, preferably 2.

About 10 minutes before baking, preheat oven to 375 degrees.

Cut dough into ¼-inch slices and place on ungreased baking sheet. Bake for 10 to 12 minutes.

PATRICIA KUCERA

Chocolate Marshmallow Slices

PHOTO ON PAGE 133

MAKES:
About 3 dozen.

FREEZEWORTHY:
Not recommended. They are crumbly and may fall apart after thawing.

NOTES

You'll need ⅓ of a box plus a few extra crackers to equal 12 ounces graham crackers, or you can use prepared graham cracker crumbs.

12 ounces graham crackers
4½ ounces semisweet chocolate, broken into pieces
½ cup (1 stick) unsalted butter
2 tablespoons superfine sugar
2 tablespoons unsweetened cocoa
2 tablespoons honey
⅔ cup mini marshmallows
½ cup white chocolate chips

Put the graham crackers in a plastic bag and, using a rolling pin, crush into small pieces.

Put the chocolate, butter, sugar, cocoa and honey in a saucepan and heat gently until chocolate and butter melt. Stir to combine. Remove from the heat and let cool slightly. Stir the crushed graham crackers into the chocolate mixture until well mixed. Add the marshmallows and mix well. Stir in the white chocolate chips.

Turn the mixture into an 8-inch square pan and lightly smooth the top. Put in the refrigerator and let chill 2 to 3 hours, until set.

GAIL SLOAN

TIP *Superfine sugar has fine grains that dissolve quicker than granulated sugar. It is often called for in drinks and no-bake cookies or bars to alleviate graininess in the final product.*

Chocolate Raisin Oaties

PHOTO ON PAGE 132

MAKES: 4 dozen.

FREEZEWORTHY: Yes, but cool completely first.

NOTES

Chocolate-covered raisins, a favorite movie treat, find their way into this oatmeal cookie recipe — with great results. You could also add or substitute chocolate-covered peanut candy.

1¼ cups all-purpose flour
1 teaspoon baking soda
¾ teaspoon ground cinnamon
½ teaspoon salt
¾ cup butter, softened
¾ cup white sugar
¾ cup packed light brown sugar
2 eggs
1 teaspoon vanilla
¾ cups rolled oats
1 cup chocolate-covered raisins

Preheat oven to 375 degrees.

Combine flour, baking soda, cinnamon and salt in a large mixing bowl. Set aside.

Cream butter and sugars in a large bowl. Beat in the eggs and vanilla until fluffy.

Gradually beat reserved flour mixture into butter mixture until well combined. Stir in oats and chocolate-covered raisins. Drop by teaspoonful onto ungreased cookie sheets.

Bake 8 to 10 minutes or until golden brown. Cool slightly; remove cookies from sheet to wire rack. Cool completely.

JANET K. KEELER

Cream Cheese Sugar Cookies

PHOTO ON PAGE 134

MAKES:
5 dozen.

FREEZEWORTHY:
Yes, but cool completely first.

NOTES

Kids love cutout cookies even if they can be difficult to make. I like to roll the dough out on parchment paper, make the cutouts, remove the excess dough, and then transfer the paper to the baking sheet. If you don't want to decorate, simply use shaped cutters such as circles and stars.

1 cup granulated sugar
1 cup (2 sticks) unsalted butter, room temperature
1 (3-ounce) package cream cheese, room temperature
½ teaspoon salt
1 teaspoon vanilla
1 egg yolk, reserve white
2 cups all-purpose flour
Colored sugars, frostings or decorations, if desired

In a large bowl, combine sugar, butter, cream cheese, salt, vanilla and egg yolk, and then blend well. Stir in flour until well blended. Refrigerate dough for 2 hours.

About 10 minutes before baking, preheat oven to 375 degrees.

On a lightly floured surface, roll out dough ⅓ at a time to ⅛-inch thickness. Cut into desired shapes with lightly floured cookie cutters. Place 2 inches apart on an ungreased cookie sheet. Leave cookies plain, or if desired, sprinkle with colored sugar. Bake for 7 to 10 minutes or until light golden brown. Cool completely.

Mini Peanut Butter Treats

PHOTO ON PAGE 134

MAKES: 3½ dozen.

FREEZEWORTHY: Yes, but cool completely first.

NOTES

Peanut butter cups meet peanut butter cookies in this treat that's fit for a children's tea party. The kids can do the stirring but an adult should work with the candies and hot dough.

½ cup (1 stick) unsalted butter, room temperature
½ cup brown sugar, packed
½ cup granulated sugar
1 egg
½ cup creamy peanut butter
½ teaspoon vanilla
1¼ cup all-purpose flour
¾ teaspoon baking soda
½ teaspoon salt

FILLING:
42 miniature peanut butter chocolate cups

Combine butter, sugars, egg, peanut butter and vanilla in mixing bowl; beat until smooth. In separate bowl, combine flour, baking soda and salt; add to creamed mixture. Cover dough and chill.

About 10 minutes before baking, preheat oven to 375 degrees.

When the dough is cold enough to handle easily, roll in small (walnut-sized) balls; place each ball in greased miniature muffin tin. Bake for 8 to 9 minutes.

Remove from oven; gently press 1 peanut butter cup into each cookie to make depression. Cool in pan 10 minutes; remove from pan and cool on rack. Store in cool place until serving time

Peanut Butter Banana Cookies

PHOTO ON PAGE 135

MAKES: About 3 dozen.

FREEZEWORTHY: Yes, but cool completely first.

NOTES

The peanut butter-banana sandwich gets turned into a sweet treat here. It's a simple recipe and a good one for beginning cooks, both young and not-so-young.

1½ cups sifted all-purpose flour
½ teaspoon baking powder
¾ teaspoon salt
¾ teaspoon cinnamon
½ cup (1 stick) unsalted butter, room temperature
½ cup peanut butter
1 cup sugar
1 egg
1 ripe banana, peeled and slightly mashed

Preheat oven to 375 degrees.

Sift together the flour, baking powder, salt and cinnamon. Set aside.

Cream the butter, peanut butter and sugar in a large mixing bowl until light and fluffy. Beat in the egg and banana.

Add the dry ingredients to the butter mixture and mix thoroughly.

Drop by teaspoonful on greased baking sheet. Bake for 8 to 10 minutes or until cookies are light brown. Cool on wire racks.

AVELINA CAPITO

TIP ***Unless you have a convection oven, bake one sheet at a time. This ensures even baking and better results.***

Fruity Cookies

PHOTO ON PAGE 132

MAKES:
About 5 dozen.

FREEZEWORTHY:
Yes, but cool completely first.

NOTES

Have the kids pick the Jell-O® flavors and get ready for some funky combinations. Lime cookies? Strawberry? Orange? Whatever their hearts desire because this is a children's recipe through and through.

4 cups all-purpose flour
1 teaspoon baking powder
1½ (3 sticks) cups butter, room temperature
1 cup sugar
1 (3-ounce) package Jell-O®, any flavor
1 egg
1 teaspoon vanilla
Additional Jell-O® or colored sugar

Preheat oven to 350 degrees.

Sift flour with baking powder in a mixing bowl. Set aside.

Cream butter in a medium mixing bowl, and then gradually add sugar and Jell-O®, creaming well after each addition. Add egg and vanilla; beat well. Gradually add flour mixture, mixing well after each addition until smooth.

Form dough into 1-inch balls and place on ungreased baking sheets. Use a glass, dipped in colored sugar or Jell-O®, to press dough flat. Sprinkle with additional Jell-O® or colored sugar, if desired.

Bake for 9 to 11 minutes or until golden brown at edges. Store in a loosely covered container.

GLENNA BOYETTE

Butterscotch Chippers

PHOTO ON PAGE 133

MAKES:
About 4 dozen.

FREEZEWORTHY:
Yes, but cool completely first.

NOTES

Enjoy this delicious change from chocolate chip cookies. Not only do they have the wondrous flavor of butterscotch, they also deliver an extra boost from oats. This is good recipe for helping hands.

1¼ cups all-purpose flour
½ teaspoon salt
½ teaspoon cinnamon
1 teaspoon baking soda
½ cup brown sugar
½ cup white sugar
1 cup (2 sticks) butter, room temperature
1 teaspoon vanilla
2 eggs
3 cups quick-cooking or old-fashioned oats
1 (12-ounce) package butterscotch chips

Preheat oven to 375 degrees.

Combine flour, salt, cinnamon, baking soda and sugars in a large bowl. Slowly mix in butter, vanilla and eggs, one ingredient at a time, incorporating well after each addition. Stir in oats and butterscotch chips until combined.

Drop by teaspoonsful onto ungreased cookie sheets and then bake 10 minutes. Remove cookies to wire racks to cool completely.

ASHLEY GORHAM

TIP ***Make sure baking sheets are completely cool before adding raw dough. If they are hot, the dough will spread too fast. To cool sheets quickly, place in freezer for about 5 minutes after you've removed hot cookies.***

Gumdrop Gems

PHOTO ON PAGE 136

MAKES:
4 dozen.

FREEZEWORTHY:
Yes, but cool completely first.

NOTES

These fun cookies can take on any color combination imaginable. Think orange and black for Halloween, red for Valentine's Day or green and red for Christmas. Gumdrops are sometimes called spice drops. Buy them smooth or with sugar coating.

2½ cups all-purpose flour
1 teaspoon baking soda
1 teaspoon cream of tartar
¼ teaspoon salt
1 cup (2 sticks) unsalted butter, room temperature
1½ cups sifted confectioners' sugar
1 teaspoon vanilla
1 egg
1 cup small gumdrops, sliced

Combine flour, baking soda, cream of tartar and salt in a mixing bowl. Set aside.

Cream together butter, sugar and vanilla; beat in the egg. Add flour mixture, beating till blended. Shape dough into two 1-inch-by-12-inch rolls; wrap in wax paper. Chill several hours or overnight.

About 10 minutes before baking, preheat oven to 350 degrees.

Cut into ¼-inch slices, keeping unsliced portion of roll chilled until needed. Place slices on ungreased cookie sheet and top with gumdrop slices. Bake for 10 minutes. Cool slightly and remove from sheet.

HEIDI BORIA

CHAPTER 5

HOLIDAY

AN ASSORTMENT OF FESTIVE GOODIES FOR ENTERTAINING AND SPECIAL TIMES

There are special memories wrapped up in the tiny treats we call cookies, and never more so than at holiday time. So many of us get warm and fuzzy feelings when we remember those afternoons spent in the kitchen with Mom or Grandma preparing once-a-year specialties. Maybe we were too young to handle the hot stuff, but measuring and stirring were always within our abilities. We would do anything to help get those cookies done quickly. And we are so happy that someone wrote those recipes down.

We may not always remember the presents we opened on Christmas morning, but the aroma of fresh-baked cookies is crystal clear. Cinnamon, molasses, peppermint, pecans and even the much-maligned candied fruit are celebrated at holiday time.

Bake a few batches of the cookies in this chapter for family and friends, but don't forget to save a few for Santa Claus. He'd appreciate an ice-cold glass of milk, too. And honestly, who wouldn't?

HOLIDAY!COOKIES

Date-Nut Krispies

PHOTO ON PAGE 140

MAKES:
About 2½ dozen.

FREEZEWORTHY:
Yes.

NOTES

These are no-bake cookies that call for an egg. If you have any health concerns about this, use a pasteurized egg instead. You'll find pasteurized egg in the same refrigerated cases as regular eggs.

½ cup (1 stick) unsalted butter, melted
1 cup sugar
1 egg, beaten
1 cup chopped dates
2 cups Rice Krispies®
½ cup chopped pecans
½ teaspoon vanilla
1 cup coconut

Mix hot butter, sugar, egg and chopped dates in pan over medium heat until thickened, stirring constantly. Cool.

Add Rice Krispies,® pecans and vanilla. With greased hands, form teaspoon-sized balls. Roll in coconut and chill.

MARY KIRKPATRICK

Walnut & Sour Cream Cookies

PHOTO ON PAGE 142

MAKES:
2½ dozen.

FREEZEWORTHY:
Yes, but cool completely first. Dust with confectioners' sugar again before serving.

NOTES

To make vanilla sugar, split 2 whole vanilla beans and bury them in a canister of confectioners' sugar. Allow the sugar to age several days before using it. You can omit this step and use plain confectioners' sugar.

1½ cups all-purpose flour
½ teaspoon baking powder
¼ teaspoon salt
¼ teaspoon ground cloves
½ cup (1 stick) unsalted butter, room temperature
⅔ cup sugar
1 large egg
1 teaspoon orange zest
1 teaspoon vanilla
6 tablespoons sour cream
¾ cup finely chopped walnuts

COATING:
1¼ cups finely chopped walnuts
¼ cup sugar
Vanilla sugar for sprinkling (see note)

Combine the flour, baking powder, salt and cloves in a mixing bowl; set aside.

Beat the butter, sugar, egg, zest and vanilla with a handheld mixer until smooth and well combined.

Turn mixer to low speed, and add the sour cream; scrape the bowl well as you work. Using a wooden spoon or a fork, stir and fold in the dry ingredients. Stir in chopped walnuts and mix thoroughly. Refrigerate dough 1 hour or longer in a covered mixing bowl.

Adjust the rack to the center position in the oven and preheat to 325 degrees. Line 2 cookie sheets with aluminum foil. Make the coating by combining the chopped nuts with the sugar in a small bowl or on wax paper.

To assemble the cookies for the oven, make tablespoon-sized balls of dough and roll in the nut and sugar coating mixture. Cover completely then flatten each ball into a chubby patty. Place on the baking sheet allowing 2 inches between each.

Bake 8 minutes. Reverse the pan so the back is in the front and bake 8 minutes longer. The cookies are done when a tester inserted comes out clean or when they spring back when pressed. Cool the cookies in the pan on a wire rack 5 minutes. Remove the cookies to a wire rack for complete cooling. Before serving, sift a shower of vanilla sugar over each cookie.

DOLORES KOSTELNI, FOOD WRITER,
LEXINGTON, VA.

Santa's Special Squares

PHOTO ON PAGE 140

MAKES:
2 dozen.

FREEZEWORTHY:
No.

NOTES

Make sure your baking pan has an edge or melted butter will spread all over the oven.

24 graham cracker squares
1 cup (2 sticks) unsalted butter
1 cup brown sugar, firmly packed
1 cup walnuts, chopped

Preheat oven to 350 degrees.

Arrange graham crackers on lightly greased 10-inch-by-15-inch jelly-roll pan. Combine butter and sugar in a 3-quart saucepan, and bring to a boil. Cook 2 minutes. Stir in nuts.

Spread mixture over graham crackers. Bake 10 minutes. Remove from pan while still warm.

Cut each square in half.

GAIL SLOAN, SUE E. CONRAD AND BEVERLY B. MILLAR

TIP *Unless you're a supremely confident baker, try out a recipe before you select it for a cookie exchange party. You don't want to be the one with the plate of store-bought treats!*

Cranberry Cherry Pinwheels

PHOTO ON PAGE 143

MAKES:
About 5½ dozen.

FREEZEWORTHY:
Yes, but let cool completely first. The dough can also be frozen and slices cut off.

NOTES

Reserve this recipe for when you have time to make the filling, roll the dough and let it chill. The end result is worth the effort because they taste as good as they look.

FILLING:
1½ cups sweetened dried cranberries
1 cup cherry preserves
½ teaspoon cinnamon
¼ cup water

DOUGH:
1 cup (2 sticks) unsalted butter, room temperature
1½ cups sugar
2 large eggs
1 tablespoon finely grated orange zest
2 teaspoons vanilla
3 cups sifted all-purpose flour
½ teaspoon baking powder
½ teaspoon salt

For filling, combine cranberries, cherry preserves and cinnamon with water in a 3-quart saucepan over medium heat. Simmer, stirring frequently, for 5 to 8 minutes, or until mixture softens and most liquid is absorbed. If it seems too dry, stir in 1 tablespoon water. Transfer to a food processor and process until smooth. Refrigerate until cool. (Filling may be stored up to 48 hours. Warm slightly and stir well before using.)

For dough, beat together butter and sugar with an electric mixer until light and fluffy, then beat in eggs, orange zest and vanilla. Sift flour, baking powder and salt into egg mixture and blend well. Chill 1 hour.

To assemble rolls, halve dough and roll out each half between sheets of waxed paper into a roughly 8-inch-by-12-inch rectangle. Remove top sheets of waxed paper (if they stick too much, chill dough briefly to firm them) and divide filling between rectangles, spreading it in an even layer. Tightly roll up each rectangle, jelly-roll fashion, beginning with a long side and using the waxed paper as an aid, to form a 12-inch log. Wrap rolls in waxed paper and then foil. Chill until firm, at least 2 hours.

Preheat oven to 350 degrees.

Working with one roll at a time (keeping the other roll chilled), remove wrapping and cut rolls crosswise into ¼-inch-thick slices and arrange slices 1 inch apart on ungreased baking sheets. Bake in batches in middle of oven until pale golden and set, 8 to 12 minutes. Transfer warm cookies to racks to cool.

KATHRYN WILSON

Nutty Cherry No-Bakes

PHOTO ON PAGE 141

MAKES: About 2 dozen.

FREEZEWORTHY: Yes.

NOTES

These are outrageously sweet, but if you like peanut butter you'll fall for them. The hidden cherry inside is a tasty surprise.

¼ cup (½ stick) unsalted butter, room temperature
½ cup peanut butter
2 cups confectioners' sugar
1 tablespoon milk
1 (10-ounce) jar maraschino cherries, well drained
5 (1-ounce) squares semisweet chocolate
2 cups walnuts, chopped

Cream butter and peanut butter with an electric mixer in a mixing bowl. Add sugar gradually and blend in milk until mixture is smooth.

Shape 1 heaping teaspoon of this mixture around each cherry.
Melt chocolate over low heat in a 2-quart saucepan. Dip balls in chocolate, roll in chopped nuts. Place on wax paper and refrigerate until set. Store in an air-tight container in the refrigerator.

JERI EMERY

TIP ***When a recipe calls for chocolate that is to be melted, be it white, milk or dark, use baking chocolate that comes in squares, not chips. Chips are formulated to keep their shape even when exposed to heat.***

Yuletide Cookie Bars

PHOTO ON PAGE 138

MAKES:
3½ to 4 dozen.

FREEZEWORTHY:
Yes, but cool completely first.

NOTES

These bars are fairly gooey so you'll have an easier time cutting them if you chill them for 30 minutes before slicing. Let cool for at least 30 minutes before putting them in the refrigerator.

FIRST LAYER:
1¼ cups all-purpose flour
1 teaspoon sugar
1 teaspoon baking powder
Dash of salt
⅔ cup cold butter
2 tablespoons cold coffee (preferred) or water
1 egg yolk (reserve egg white)
1 (12-ounce) package semisweet chocolate morsels

SECOND LAYER:
½ cup (1 stick) unsalted butter, room temperature
1 cup sugar
1 tablespoon vanilla
2 eggs plus reserved egg white
1 cup raisins
1 cup walnuts, chopped
Confectioners' sugar

Preheat oven to 350 degrees.

To prepare the bottom layer, combine flour, sugar, baking powder and salt in a mixing bowl. Cut in butter until mixture resembles coarse meal. Set aside. Blend together coffee and egg yolk in a small bowl. Stir coffee mixture into flour mixture; moisten evenly. Bring dough together enough to form a ball. With floured fingertips, press evenly onto bottom of greased 10-inch-by-15-inch jelly roll pan (layer will be thin). Bake for 10 minutes. Sprinkle chocolate morsels evenly over crust; return to oven for 2 minutes to melt chocolate. Remove from oven; spread chocolate evenly with spatula. Let stand several minutes to set.

To prepare the top layer, cream butter in a large mixing bowl. Beat in sugar and vanilla, then eggs and egg white, one at a time (mixture may look curdled). Stir in raisins and walnuts. Spread mixture evenly over bottom layer. Return to oven; bake 20 to 25 minutes, until top is browned. Dust with confectioners' sugar. Cool, and then cut into bars.

SUE E. CONRAD

Snowball Surprises

PHOTO ON PAGE 143

MAKES:
3 dozen

FREEZEWORTHY:
They'll stay softer if not frozen.

NOTES

Freeze the chocolate Hershey's Kisses® before wrapping the dough around them and they'll keep their shape better in the oven.

1 cup (2 sticks) unsalted butter, room temperature
1 teaspoon vanilla
1¾ cups all-purpose flour
1 cup finely chopped walnuts
½ cup sugar
1 (6-ounce package) chocolate Hershey's Kisses®
Confectioners' sugar

Blend first five ingredients well in a large mixing bowl. Refrigerate for 1 hour until dough is firm.

About 10 minutes before baking, preheat oven to 375 degrees.

Wrap enough dough around each unwrapped kiss to cover completely, and shape into a ball. Place on cookie sheet and bake for 12 minutes. Roll in confectioners' sugar while still warm. Store in an air-tight container.

DEBORAH SURMAN-HOBBS

TIP **Most cookie dough freezes well and can be kept for up to three months. It's best to wrap it twice and secure well to prevent freezer burn.**

Holiday Raisin Walnut Bars

PHOTO ON PAGE 141

MAKES:
16 bars.

FREEZEWORTHY:
No, the soft second layer will cause the bars to crumble after thawing.

NOTES

Remove these bars from the pan carefully because the jam layer is soft. Larger squares could be served with a scoop of vanilla ice cream. No matter how you serve them, they're a delicate treat packed with flavor. Yum!

FIRST LAYER:
1¼ cups all-purpose flour
⅓ cup sugar
½ cup (1 stick) unsalted butter, room temperature

SECOND LAYER:
1 cup chopped raisins
¾ cup raspberry or plum jam

THIRD LAYER:
2 eggs
¾ cup brown sugar
¼ cup flour
¼ teaspoon baking powder
¼ teaspoon salt
1 cup chopped walnuts
1 teaspoon orange zest
1 teaspoon vanilla
Confectioners' sugar

Preheat oven to 350 degrees.

To make the first layer, combine the three ingredients and blend into fine crumbs. Press firmly into bottom of greased 8-inch-square pan. Bake for 25 minutes, or until edges are lightly browned.

To make the second layer, mix together raisins and jam; spread over shortbread base.

To make the third layer, beat eggs with brown sugar, flour, baking powder and salt; stir in walnuts, orange zest and vanilla. Pour mixture evenly over jam layer.

Bake 35 to 40 minutes, or until top is brown and springs back when lightly touched. Cool in pan. Sift confectioners' sugar over top.

ANDREA ROCKMAN

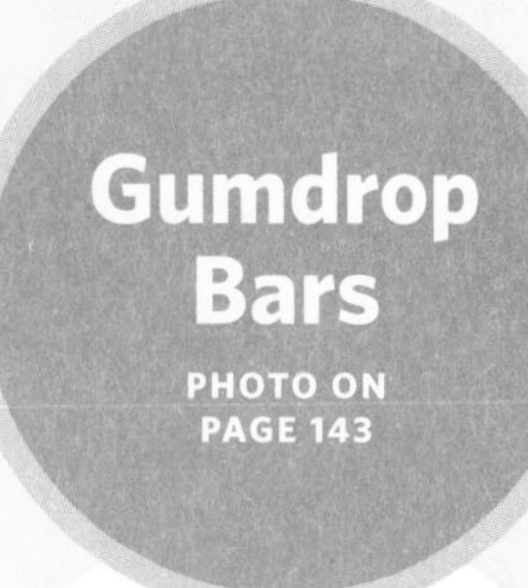

Gumdrop Bars

PHOTO ON PAGE 143

MAKES:
30 thin bars.

FREEZEWORTHY:
No.

NOTES

Select bright and pretty holiday colors for these festive treats. To decorate bars, arrange one drop cut in half on top of the icing.

½ cup sugared or plain gumdrops, cut into small pieces
½ cup chopped nuts
1 cup plus 1½ teaspoons all-purpose flour, divided use
⅛ teaspoon salt
½ teaspoon cinnamon
1 cup brown sugar
2 eggs
2 tablespoons evaporated milk
Vanilla frosting, store-bought or homemade

Preheated oven to 325 degrees.

Stir gumdrop pieces with nuts and 1½ teaspoons flour to coat. Set aside.

Sift together 1 cup of flour, salt and cinnamon. To this, add brown sugar, eggs and evaporated milk; mix well. Add gumdrop mixture and beat well until incorporated. (Batter will be thick.) Spread the batter into a well-greased 9-inch baking pan. Bake for 35 minutes. Cool.

Ice with vanilla frosting. Cut into 3-inch-by-1-inch squares and decorate with gumdrops.

JOHN PACHECO

TIP ***If you're transporting bar cookies, cut, store and carry them in the pan in which they are baked. Remove and arrange them on a serving platter once you get to your destination.***

Grand Marnier® Wreaths

PHOTO ON PAGE 142

MAKES: 2 dozen.

FREEZEWORTHY: Yes.

NOTES

These are a bit fussy but they scream "Christmas!" Take your time and roll the dough into precise 5-inch pieces before shaping into wreaths. The care you take will pay off in cookies that are lovely to look at.

2¼ cups all-purpose flour
1 teaspoon ground nutmeg
¼ teaspoon salt
⅔ cup unsalted butter, room temperature
⅓ cup sugar
2 tablespoons grated orange rind
1 egg
2 tablespoons Grand Marnier® liqueur
¼ cup candied red cherries, chopped

GLAZE:
1¼ cups sifted confectioners' sugar
1 tablespoon Grand Marnier® liqueur
⅛ teaspoon ground nutmeg
1 tablespoon milk

Preheat oven to 350 degrees. Grease cookie sheets.

Sift flour, nutmeg and salt in bowl.

Beat together butter, sugar and orange rind in large bowl until light and fluffy. Beat in egg and liqueur until smooth. Stir in flour mixture until well blended. Gently stir in chopped cherries.

Using 1 tablespoon of dough for each cookie, roll into a 5-inch-long rope. Shape each rope into a wreath and place wreaths on greased cookie sheets 2 inches apart.

Bake 10 to 12 minutes until lightly browned at edges. Transfer to rack to cool.

To make the glaze, blend glaze ingredients in small bowl until smooth and of good spreading consistency. Add milk, as needed.

Spread glaze lightly over cooled cookies. Decorate with red and green cherries to look like wreaths.

BARBARA MCGEEVER

Molasses Crinkles

PHOTO ON PAGE 139

MAKES:
4 to 5 dozen.

FREEZEWORTHY:
Yes, but cool completely first.

NOTES

Sticky-sweet molasses provides deep flavor here, while cloves, cinnamon and ginger lend the holiday touch.

¾ cup shortening
1 cup brown sugar
1 egg
4 tablespoons molasses
2¼ cups all-purpose flour
¼ teaspoon salt
2 teaspoons baking soda
½ teaspoon cloves
1 teaspoon cinnamon
1 teaspoon ginger
Granulated sugar, for rolling

Preheat oven to 350 degrees. Spray baking sheet with nonstick spray.

Blend all ingredients except granulated sugar in a bowl until thoroughly mixed. Shape into balls the size of a quarter. Roll the balls in granulated sugar before placing on baking sheet. Do not flatten.

Bake for 12 to 15 minutes until cracked on top and firm to the touch.

RONALD CONRADT

TIP ***Baking soda and baking powder are not the same thing and are not interchangeable even though both are leavening agents. Baking soda needs an acid, such as citrus juice or buttermilk, to activate it. Baking powder includes the acid. Always use the one called for.***

Candy Cane Gingersnaps

PHOTO ON PAGE 141

MAKES: About 3 dozen.

FREEZEWORTHY: Yes, but cool completely first.

NOTES

Ground, fresh and crystallized ginger provides these snaps with a triple-power punch. The crushed candy cane sprinkling on top makes them especially suited for Christmas.

2 cups all-purpose flour
2 teaspoons baking soda
¾ teaspoon kosher salt
1 teaspoon ground cinnamon
1 teaspoon ground ginger
¼ teaspoon ground allspice
¼ teaspoon ground cloves
½ cup (1 stick) unsalted butter, room temperature
1 cup granulated sugar
¼ cup dark molasses
1 egg
1-inch piece fresh ginger, peeled and grated
3 ounces crystallized ginger, chopped coarsely
3 ounces peppermint candy canes
Granulated sugar for sprinkling

Combine flour, baking soda, salt, cinnamon, ginger, allspice and cloves in a medium mixing bowl, mix well. Set aside.

Combine butter, sugar, molasses, egg and fresh ginger in a large mixing bowl; mix well. Add dry ingredients to wet ingredients and mix until well combined; stir in crystallized ginger. Wrap dough in wax paper and place in refrigerator for at least 1 hour.

Place candy canes in a heavy plastic bag and break into small pieces, using either a mallet or rolling pin.

About 10 minutes before baking, preheat oven to 375 degrees.

Portion out chilled dough by heaping tablespoons, forming into balls if you wish, and place 2 inches apart on ungreased cookie sheet. Flatten each cookie slightly. Bake 8 to 10 minutes. Remove from oven and immediately sprinkle each cookie with a few pieces of broken candy cane and granulated sugar. Cool.

APRIL LEROY

Retro Jewel Cookies

PHOTO ON PAGE 138

MAKES:
3 to 4 dozen.

FREEZEWORTHY:
So-so results. This is a soft cookie that will be even softer after thawing.

NOTES

Retro Jewel Cookies are a fruit-cake lover's dream. They will adore these gems. And detractors? Well, they just might be converted!

1 cup shortening
2 cups dark brown sugar
2 eggs
½ cup buttermilk (or ½ cup milk mixed with 1 teaspoon lemon juice)
3½ cups all-purpose flour
1½ teaspoons baking soda
1 teaspoon salt
2 cups chopped pecans
2 cups chopped candied cherries
2 cups chopped dates

Preheat oven to 300 degrees.

Combine shortening, sugar, eggs and buttermilk in a mixing bowl; beat well. Sift flour, baking soda and salt together. Stir into shortening mixture; mix well. Add pecans, cherries and dates, mixing well.

Drop by tablespoonsful onto greased cookie sheet. Bake for 12 to 15 minutes, until light brown in color. Remove from cookie sheet and cool on wire racks.

Store in container with a tight-fitting lid; cookies keep well at least a week.

GERRY CAMERON

TIP *Eggs should be at room temperature. Cold eggs can cause melted chocolate to get lumpy or softened butter to firm up unexpectedly, creating tough cookies. To bring eggs to room temperature, set them out on the counter while the oven is preheating.*

Peppermint Fudgies

PHOTO ON PAGE 143

MAKES:
40 to 45 cookies.

FREEZEWORTHY:
So-so results. This soft cookie will be even softer when thawed.

NOTES

These cookies are so decadent and delightful that everyone has a tough time waiting for them to cool before they start grabbing samples. They just might be gone before their time!

2 cups (12-ounce) semisweet chocolate morsels, divided use
4 tablespoons (½ stick) unsalted butter
1 (14-ounce) can sweetened condensed milk
6 tablespoons finely crushed peppermint candy, divided use
1 large egg
¼ teaspoon peppermint or ½ teaspoon vanilla
1 cup all-purpose flour
5 tablespoons unsweetened cocoa powder

Position a rack in the middle of the oven and preheat to 350 degrees.

Line several baking sheets with parchment or aluminum foil. In a large microwave-safe bowl, microwave 1 cup chocolate morsels and the butter on full power for 1 minute. Stir well. Continue microwaving on medium power, stopping and stirring at 30-second intervals. Stop microwaving before the chocolate completely melts and let the residual heat finish the job.

Stir the sweetened condensed milk, half the crushed candy, the egg and peppermint (or vanilla) extract into the chocolate mixture until blended. In a medium bowl, stir together the flour and cocoa. Stir the flour mixture into the chocolate mixture until blended. Stir in the remaining 1 cup chocolate morsels. If the dough seems too soft to drop, let stand for 5 minutes to firm slightly.

Drop the dough by heaping measuring tablespoonsful, or use a small ice cream scoop lightly coated with nonstick spray, on the baking sheets, spacing the cookies 2 inches apart. Bake one sheet at a time for 6 to 9 minutes, or until the centers are almost firm when pressed. Do not over bake.

Remove from the oven and garnish each cookie with a pinch or two of the remaining crushed candy. Bake for 1 to 2 minutes longer, or until the candy bits begin to melt. Transfer the sheet to a wire rack to cool for 5 minutes. Using a spatula, transfer cookies to the rack to cool completely.

NANCY BAGGETT, COOKBOOK AUTHOR

Snow Topped Mint Bars

PHOTO ON PAGE 140

MAKES: About 3 dozen.

FREEZEWORTHY: No.

To smash peppermint candies, I use two plastic bags, one filled with candy and nestled inside an empty one so that the sharp edges of the smashed pieces don't poke through.

1 cup (2 sticks) unsalted butter, room temperature
⅔ cup sugar
1 egg
1 teaspoon vanilla
2 cups all-purpose flour, divided
½ cup milk
⅓ cup crushed peppermint candy or candy canes
Confectioners' sugar

Preheat oven to 375 degrees. Grease and flour a 9-inch-by-13-inch baking pan.

Cream butter and sugar in a large mixing bowl until light colored and fluffy. Beat in egg and vanilla. Add 1 cup flour, mix well, and then add milk. Incorporate remaining cup of flour. Beat well for 2 to 3 minutes.

Stir in crushed peppermint candies and pour into prepared pan. Bake in center of oven 20 to 25 minutes.

Cool completely, and then sprinkle with confectioners' sugar. Cut into bars.

GALE RUST

TIP *In general, cool cookies completely before rolling in confectioners' sugar. If they are hot or even warm, they will absorb the sugar and it will disappear.*

NOTES

Cherry Squares

PHOTO ON PAGE 139

MAKES:
About 16 squares.

FREEZEWORTHY:
No, the icing will weep when thawed.

NOTES

These festive squares, though delicious, are very rich. You may be able to get more than 16 squares from the pan. Also, drain the cherries well on paper towels so the juice doesn't stain the icing.

FIRST LAYER:
1¼ cups all-purpose flour
⅓ cup firmly packed light brown sugar
½ cup (1 stick) unsalted butter, cut into cubes

SECOND LAYER:
2 large eggs
1¼ cups firmly packed light brown sugar
1 tablespoon all-purpose flour
½ teaspoon baking powder
1 cup flaked coconut
½ cup chopped walnuts
½ cup maraschino cherries, cut up

ICING:
1 cup confectioners' sugar
2 tablespoons butter
½ teaspoon vanilla
1 tablespoon milk
Cherry juice or red food coloring (optional)

Preheat oven to 350 degrees.

For first layer, cut butter into flour and brown sugar until crumbs form. Press into ungreased 9-inch pan. Bake for 15 minutes.

For second layer, beat eggs slightly and add the rest of the ingredients in the order given. Spread over first layer. Return to oven and bake for 25 minutes or until brown.

For icing, beat together ingredients in small bowl and spread over cooled squares. If you want the icing to remain white, leave out the cherry juice or food coloring.

SHARON LAROCK

Pumpkin Drop Cookies

PHOTO ON PAGE 140

MAKES:
3 dozen.

FREEZEWORTHY:
Yes, but cool completely first.

NOTES

Make sure you buy 100 percent pure pumpkin and not pumpkin pie filling for this recipe. You want the flavor of pumpkin but not the added sweetness of pie filling.

½ cup shortening
1 cup brown sugar
2 eggs
1 cup canned pumpkin puree
2 cups all-purpose flour
4 teaspoons baking powder
1 teaspoon salt
1 tablespoon pumpkin pie spice
⅔ to ¾ cup raisins
1 (10-ounce) jar maraschino cherries, drained well and chopped
6 ounces semisweet chocolate chips

Preheat oven to 350 degrees.

Blend together shortening and sugar. Add eggs and pumpkin, and mix well. Sift flour, baking powder, salt and pumpkin pie spice and then slowly add to shortening mixture, stirring (or mixing) well after each addition. Stir in raisins, cherries and chocolate chips.

Drop by teaspoonful onto greased cookie sheets. Bake for 15 minutes. Cool 1 minute before removing cookies from cookie sheet.

KATHY SEBEST

TIP *Cookie dough is mixed in stages for important reasons. Butter and sugar are creamed together first to add lightness and lift to the finished cookie. Follow the mixing directions exactly for best results.*

White Christmas Shortbread

PHOTO ON PAGE 141

MAKES:
3 to 4 dozen.

FREEZEWORTHY:
With reservations. The icing might weep a bit when thawed.

NOTES

This recipe originally called for seeds from a vanilla bean, but we find the extract a more economical ingredient. Also, this is a wet dough. Do not be alarmed as it will firm nicely in the refrigerator.

2 cups (4 sticks) unsalted butter, room temperature
1 cup light brown sugar, packed
1 teaspoon vanilla
4½ cups sifted all-purpose flour

BROWN BUTTER ICING:
6 tablespoons butter
3 cups sifted confectioners' sugar
1 teaspoon vanilla
3 tablespoons milk
Colored sugar for sprinkling

Cream together butter and sugar in a large mixing bowl. Add vanilla. Mix in flour until just incorporated.

Turn out dough onto floured work surface. Knead for 5 minutes. Dough should be smooth and just barely sticky. Roll dough into two logs (about 12 inches long and 2 inches around) and wrap with plastic wrap. Chill for 2 hours.

Preheat oven to 325 degrees.

Working quickly so the dough doesn't get soft, slice dough into ⅓-inch to ½-inch discs. Place on parchment-lined baking sheet and prick discs with fork three times. Bake for 20 minutes. Watch the cookies carefully and take them out when the edges start to turn golden. Do not over bake. Let cool for a few minutes, then transfer to wire racks.

To prepare icing, melt butter in a 10-inch skillet over medium-high heat until it turns light brown (a golden tan color). Pour brown butter over confectioners' sugar and beat with an electric mixer until fluffy. Add vanilla; then add milk one tablespoon at a time until you reach the right spreading consistency. Ice cookies immediately and sprinkle with colored sugar.

HEATHER GREENWAY

Sitting Pretties

PHOTO ON PAGE 138

MAKES:
About 3 dozen.

FREEZEWORTHY:
So-so results. If you must freeze, do it before adding frosting and candy.

NOTES

This is a frosted twist on the traditional thumbprint cookies with colorful candies providing the decoration. Change up the colors for any holiday.

1 cup (2 sticks) unsalted butter, room temperature
½ cup packed light brown sugar
2 eggs, separated
1 teaspoon vanilla
2 cups all-purpose flour
½ teaspoon salt
Finely chopped nuts

DECORATION:
1 (16-ounce) can vanilla frosting or 2 cups homemade vanilla frosting
Red and green plain or peanut M&M's®

Cream butter and brown sugar in a large mixing bowl. Add egg yolks and vanilla. Blend flour and salt into mixture. Cover and chill dough 1 hour.

About 10 minutes before baking, preheat oven to 350 degrees.

Roll dough into 1-inch balls. Dip each into egg whites that have been beaten slightly. Roll in nuts. Place balls 1 inch apart on ungreased cookie sheets. Bake for 5 minutes. Remove from oven. Gently press your thumb, or use a thimble, to make an indentation in center of each cookie, creating a shallow well.

Return to oven and bake 5 more minutes. Cool. Fill indentation generously with frosting and decorate with red or green M&M's.®

NANCY J. STOHS, FOOD EDITOR,
MILWAUKEE JOURNAL SENTINEL

Gingerbread Bars

PHOTO ON PAGE 139

MAKES:
About 36 squares.

FREEZEWORTHY:
Yes. Freeze in the pan after they are cooled and before they are cut.

NOTES

I imagine these bars as the perfect offering after an afternoon holiday luncheon. They bring together all the flavors of the season in one simple treat.

2¾ cups all-purpose flour
1¼ teaspoons salt
1¼ teaspoons baking soda
1½ teaspoons ground ginger
1½ teaspoons cinnamon
¼ teaspoon ground cloves
1¼ cups (2½ sticks) unsalted butter, room temperature
1¼ cups light brown sugar, firmly packed
½ cup plus 2 tablespoons white sugar
2 large eggs plus 1 egg yolk
1½ teaspoons vanilla
⅓ cup molasses
1 cup toasted chopped pecans
Confectioners' sugar for dusting

Preheat oven to 350 degrees.

Grease a 9-inch-by-13-inch baking pan and line bottom with greased parchment paper. Or, line entire pan with nonstick aluminum foil.

Combine flour, salt, baking soda, ginger, cinnamon and cloves in a medium bowl. Set aside.

Beat butter and sugars in a large bowl with electric mixer on high speed for 3 minutes. Add eggs and yolk, one at a time, combining well after each addition Add vanilla and molasses, and mix on medium speed until combined. Stir in flour mixture, combining gently with a large spoon. Gently fold in pecans.

Spread batter evenly in pan and bake about 30 to 35 minutes, until edges just begin to harden. Cool completely in the pan before cutting into squares. Dust with confectioners' sugar if you'd like.

HELENE GOLD

Candied Fruit Slices

PHOTO ON PAGE 140

MAKES: 7 dozen.

FREEZEWORTHY: Yes, but cool completely first.

NOTES

These little jewels are fun to make and pretty to look at. The fact that they are slice-and-bakes makes them convenient for busy cooks. Keep the dough tightly wrapped in the freezer and you can bake as many or as few as you'd like.

1 cup (2 sticks) unsalted butter, room temperature
1 cup confectioners' sugar
1 egg
1 teaspoon vanilla
2¼ cups all-purpose flour
½ teaspoon baking soda
1 cup pecan halves
1 cup soft candied green cherries, cut in half
1 cup soft candied red cherries, cut in half

Cream butter and confectioners' sugar in a large mixing bowl. Add egg and vanilla, and then mix well. Mix in flour and baking soda to make a smooth dough. Stir in pecans and candied cherries until evenly incorporated.

Chill dough for 1 hour, and then divide into 4 portions. Roll each piece into a log about 7 inches long and 1½ inches around. Wrap in wax paper and chill for at least 3 hours.

About 10 minutes before baking, preheat oven to 350 degrees.

Unwrap rolls and slice about ⅛-inch thick. Bake on ungreased cookie sheet for 13 to 15 minutes or until lightly browned.

JEAN GIBSON AND JOANNE H. STAATS

TIP *To make chopping dried fruit easier, coat the blade of a heavy chef's knife with nonstick cooking spray. Or, use kitchen shears to snip the fruit apart.*

Peppermint Wands

PHOTO ON PAGE 141

MAKES:
About 7 dozen.

FREEZEWORTHY:
Yes, and they are even delicious frozen!

NOTES

Fans of the fussy twisted peppermint candy cane cookies might find a good substitute here. This is a tender dough and works better when the cookies are small. We use candy canes for decoration. They are easier to crush than peppermint candies.

2 cups all-purpose flour
⅛ teaspoon baking powder
¼ teaspoon salt
1 cup (2 sticks) unsalted butter, room temperature
1 cup confectioners' sugar
2 teaspoons vanilla

COATING:
4 ounces German sweet chocolate, melted
10 red and white peppermints (or candy canes), crushed, or finely chopped nuts

Combine flour, baking powder and salt in bowl; set aside. Beat butter and confectioners' sugar in large bowl until light and fluffy. Beat in vanilla. On low speed, beat in flour mixture until combined. Refrigerate 30 minutes.

About 10 minutes before baking, preheat oven to 350 degrees. Line baking sheet with aluminum foil.

Roll 1 teaspoon of dough into a log, about 2½ inches long. Place on prepared baking sheet. Repeat with remaining dough, placing cookies 1½ inches apart. Bake for 10 to 12 minutes or until very pale golden at edges. Remove cookies to wire racks to cool.

To make the coating, work with cool cookies, dipping one end of each cookie into melted chocolate. Return to wire rack. Sprinkle each dipped end with ¼ teaspoon crushed peppermints or finely chopped nuts. Cool on racks in refrigerator for 20 minutes to set. Store in air-tight containers at room temperature.

MARION HAUPT

MAKES:
About 6 dozen.

FREEZEWORTHY:
Yes, but cool completely first.

NOTES

Shredded coconut on the outside of these cookies is a sweet nod to St. Nick's beard. They are fun for kids to help bake and easy for everyone because they are slice-and-bakes.

1 cup (2 sticks) unsalted butter, room temperature
1 cup sugar
2 tablespoons milk
1 teaspoon vanilla or ½ teaspoon rum extract
2½ cups all-purpose flour
¾ cup finely chopped red and/or green candied cherries
¾ cup finely chopped pecans
¾ cup shredded coconut

Beat butter in a large bowl with an electric mixer on medium to high speed for 30 seconds. Add sugar and beat until fluffy. Add milk and vanilla or rum extract; beat well.

Add flour and beat until well mixed. Stir in cherries and pecans. Divide dough into thirds. Shape each portion into a 7-inch-long log. Roll each log in ¼ cup of the coconut to coat. Wrap and chill in the refrigerator at least 2 hours or up to 24 hours.

About 10 minutes before baking, preheat oven to 375 degrees. Cut dough into ¼-inch-thick slices. Place on an ungreased cookie sheet. Bake for 10 to 12 minutes or until edges are lightly browned. Cool cookies on wire rack.

KATHRYN REM, FOOD EDITOR,
STATE JOURNAL-REGISTER, SPRINGFIELD, ILL.

TIP **When baking cookies for a party or friends, make an extra batch for your own family. This is an especially good idea for cookies that freeze well.**

Orange Spice Gems

PHOTO ON PAGE 142

MAKES:
3½ dozen.

FREEZEWORTHY:
Yes, but cookies will be softer when thawed. Cool completely before freezing.

NOTES

The cake mix is the easy first step in making these citrus and liqueur spiked cookies. They make a delightful winter offering when oranges are at their peak.

3½ cups sifted spice cake mix
1 teaspoon cinnamon
1 medium apple, peeled and diced
1 tablespoon orange zest
2 teaspoons Grand Marnier®, optional
1 cup dried cranberries
Juice from 1 medium orange
½ cup (1 stick) unsalted butter, room temperature
2 eggs
1 cup chopped pecans

GLAZE:
1 cup confectioners' sugar
3 to 4 tablespoons orange juice

Preheat oven to 350 degrees.

Combine cake mix, cinnamon, apples, orange zest and Grand Marnier®, if using, in a mixing bowl. Set aside. Combine cranberries and orange juice in a separate bowl; set aside. In another bowl, mix butter with eggs; add to cake-mix mixture until thoroughly blended and then add cranberry-orange juice combination. Mix well.

Drop dough by half-tablespoons 1 inch apart on parchment-lined baking sheets. Sprinkle with pecans. Bake for 15 minutes. Let cool before removing from cookie sheet. To make the glaze, mix together confectioners' sugar and orange juice until mixture can be drizzled over tops of cookies. The cookies will be cakelike.

ELAINE PATENAUDE AND VERNIE FRIGERI

Candy Cane Puffs

PHOTO ON PAGE 139

MAKES:
4 dozen.

FREEZEWORTHY:
No. These are better eaten soon after being made.

NOTES

A bit of red food coloring in the melted white chocolate makes the puffs look like they've been baked by Santa's elves. Candy Cane Puffs are favorites among kids and kids-at-heart.

2½ cups all-purpose flour
¼ teaspoon salt
½ cup (1 stick) unsalted butter, room temperature
1 cup confectioners' sugar
1 egg
½ teaspoon peppermint extract
½ teaspoon vanilla
8 ounces white chocolate baking pieces, melted
½ cup finely chopped candy canes

Stir together flour and salt in medium-size bowl. Set aside.

Beat butter and sugar in large bowl until smooth and creamy. Beat in egg. Beat in peppermint extract and vanilla.

On low speed, beat in flour mixture until smooth dough is formed. Wrap dough in plastic wrap; refrigerate 1 hour.

About 10 minutes before baking, preheat oven to 375 degrees.

Shape dough into 1-inch balls; place on lightly greased baking sheets. Bake for 10 to 12 minutes or until bottoms are lightly browned; cookie tops will not be brown at all. Transfer cookies to wire racks to cool completely.

Brush melted white chocolate on top and sprinkle with crushed candy canes.

PEGGY KATALINICH, FOOD EDITOR,
FAMILY CIRCLE MAGAZINE

TIP ***Heat-resistant spatulas are good for scraping mixing bowls and stirring chocolate or butter as it melts.***

Dipped Gingersnaps

PHOTO ON PAGE 139

MAKES:
3 to 4 dozen.

FREEZEWORTHY:
Yes, but let melted chocolate harden first.

NOTES

I love these cookies because they turn out perfect every time I make them. Dipping half the cookie into melted white chocolate makes them oh-so special. And did I mention they are delicious?

2 cups sugar
1½ cups vegetable oil
2 eggs
½ cup molasses
4 cups all-purpose flour
4 teaspoons baking soda
1 tablespoon ground ginger
2 teaspoons ground cinnamon
1 teaspoon salt
Additional sugar for rolling

COATING:
2 (12-ounce) packages white chocolate chips
¼ cup shortening

Preheat oven to 350 degrees.

Combine sugar and oil in a large bowl; mix well. Add eggs, one at a time, beating well after each addition. Stir in molasses. Combine dry ingredients in separate bowl; gradually add to creamed mixture and mix well. Shape into ¾-inch balls and roll in sugar. Place 2 inches apart on ungreased baking sheet and bake for 10 to 12 minutes. Remove from cookie sheet to cool.

Melt chips or bark and shortening in microwave-safe bowl at the medium or 50 percent setting for 30 seconds adding additional seconds if required. Stir until smooth. Dip cookies halfway into the warm dip and place on waxed paper to set.

JANET STARR

Cathedral Cookies

PHOTO ON PAGE 139

MAKES:
2 dozen.

FREEZEWORTHY:
No.

NOTES

Mini colored marshmallows make these festive cookies look like stained-glass windows. They are best eaten soon after being removed from the refrigerator because they get soft quickly.

12 ounces chocolate chips
½ cup (1 stick) unsalted butter
2 eggs (see note)
½ cup chopped nuts
1 (10-ounce) package colored mini marshmallows
Confectioners' sugar

Melt chips and butter in a medium saucepan. Add eggs and nuts. Cool completely (will take about 20 minutes), then gradually add marshmallows.

Meanwhile, sprinkle confectioners' sugar on 3 pieces of wax paper. Divide cookie mixture into 3 parts and place on the wax paper. Add more confectioners' sugar to tops, roll, wrap and twist paper ends to secure. They will resemble three logs.

Refrigerate overnight, slice and serve.

NOTE: These are no-bake cookies, but the raw eggs should be heated enough to kill bacteria when they are mixed with the hot melted chocolate chips and butter. Egg substitute can be used if you are concerned.

JAYNE LALIBERTE

Cranberry Orange Cookies

PHOTO ON PAGE 143

MAKES:
5 dozen.

FREEZEWORTHY:
Yes, but cool completely first.

NOTES

The surprising addition of chopped candy orange slices gives these cookies extra pizzazz. They are an excellent choice for a cookie exchange because they travel well.

1½ cups firmly packed brown sugar
1 cup (2 sticks) unsalted butter, room temperature
1 teaspoon vanilla
2 eggs
2¼ cups all-purpose flour
2 teaspoons baking powder
1 teaspoon baking soda
½ teaspoon salt
2 cups rolled oats
1 cup sweetened dried cranberries
1 cup chopped orange-slice candies

GLAZE:
¾ cup confectioners' sugar
2 to 3 teaspoons orange juice

Preheat oven to 350 degrees.

Combine brown sugar and butter in a large bowl; beat until light and fluffy. Add vanilla and eggs and blend well. Add flour, baking powder, baking soda and salt; mix well. Stir in oats, cranberries and chopped candies. Drop dough by rounded teaspoonsful 2 inches apart onto ungreased cookie sheets.

Bake for 9 to 11 minutes or until golden brown. Cool 1 minute; remove from cookie sheets to racks. Cool completely, about 15 minutes more.

In a small bowl, combine glaze ingredients, adding enough orange juice for desired drizzling consistency. Drizzle glaze over cooled cookies.

GAYLE HACKBARTH

Peppermint Pinwheels

PHOTO ON PAGE 138

MAKES:
About 3 dozen.

FREEZEWORTHY:
Yes, but cool completely first.

NOTES

Peppermint Pinwheels are pretty to look at and even better to eat. Read the recipe through at least once before you start. The dough must be chilled twice.

1 cup (2 sticks) unsalted butter, room temperature
1 cup sifted confectioners' sugar
1 egg
2½ cups sifted all-purpose flour
1 teaspoon salt
1½ teaspoons vanilla
½ teaspoon red food coloring
¼ cup each finely crushed peppermint-stick candy and sugar

Mix butter, sugar, egg and flavorings in a mixing bowl, combining well. Mix in flour and salt, and blend in thoroughly.

When a smooth dough forms, divide in half. Blend food coloring into one half, and then chill both halves until firm.

On lightly floured cloth-covered board, roll the plain half into a 12-inch square. Roll the red half the same size and lay on top of the plain dough. Roll the double-layered dough gently until about ¼- inch thick. Roll up like a jelly roll and chill one hour.

About 10 minutes before baking, preheat oven to 375 degrees.

Slice cookies ¼-inch thick. Place on ungreased baking sheet and bake 9 minutes, or until lightly browned. While still warm, brush with egg white glaze (1 egg white combined with 2 tablespoons water) and sprinkle with peppermint candy and sugar.

RUTH NELSON

TIP ***Ice cream scoops come in several sizes and are perfect for measuring drop cookies uniformly.***

Cherry Nut Slices

PHOTO ON PAGE 142

MAKES:
6 to 7 dozen.

FREEZEWORTHY:
Yes, but cool completely first.

NOTES

If you can't find Brazil nuts, use whole almonds that are toasted and chopped. To toast almonds, stir them in a dry skillet over medium heat until you smell their aroma. Remove from pan immediately. Cool.

8 ounces candied red cherries, whole
1¾ cups sifted all-purpose flour
½ teaspoon salt
½ teaspoon cinnamon
¼ teaspoon baking soda
¾ cup (1½ sticks) unsalted butter, room temperature
½ cup packed light brown sugar
½ teaspoon vanilla
2 tablespoons milk
¾ cups walnuts, chopped
½ cup Brazil nuts, chopped

Drain cherries and spread on paper towels; pat with additional paper towel to remove the sticky syrup. Set aside. Sift flour with salt, cinnamon and baking soda into a mixing bowl. Set aside.

Cream butter. Add brown sugar, vanilla and milk, beating until smooth. Add flour mixture gradually, beating thoroughly after each addition. Stir in cherries and chopped nuts. Divide dough and shape into 2 rolls, 12-inches long. (If too sticky to handle, refrigerate dough for 30 minutes before shaping.) Wrap in waxed paper. Chill 4 to 6 hours or overnight.

About 10 minutes before baking, preheat oven to 350 degrees.

Cut into ¼-inch slices and place cookies on ungreased cookie sheet or parchment paper-lined sheet. Bake 10 to 12 minutes, or until golden.

KAREN SHAMPAINE

INDEX!

A-B

C

D-F

G-L

M-O

P-R

S-Z